SURROUNDED BY INSANITY

SURROUNDED

BY

INSANITY

HOW TO EXECUTE BAD DECISIONS

DONALD MEADOR

THE CORPORATE MIDDLE PUBLISHING

COPYRIGHT © 2019 DONALD MEADOR
All rights reserved.

SURROUNDED BY INSANITY
How to Execute Bad Decisions

ISBN 978-1-5445-0267-0 *Hardcover*
978-1-5445-0265-6 *Paperback*
978-1-5445-0266-3 *Ebook*

To all the corporate minions who suffer in silence
at the hands of others' incompetence.

CONTENTS

ACKNOWLEDGMENTS ～～～～～ 9

INTRODUCTION ～～～～～～～ 11

1. YOU HAVE ALREADY LOST ～～～～ 21

2. MANAGE YOUR BOSS ～～～～～ 39

3. FIND THE CRACKS ～～～～～ 61

4. MANAGE YOUR TEAM ～～～～ 75

5. INSULATE YOURSELF FROM THE RESULTS ～～ 91

6. REALITY IS IRRELEVANT ～～～～ 107

7. WHAT IF YOU ARE WRONG? ～～～ 123

8. THIS WILL HAPPEN AGAIN ～～～ 139

9. MANAGE YOURSELF ～～～～～ 155

10. CONCLUSION ～～～～～～～ 165

ABOUT THE AUTHOR ～～～～～ 177

ACKNOWLEDGMENTS

I have to begin with wholeheartedly thanking my wife, Rebecca. Writing a book is a long, time-consuming process and she was right there beside me supporting me and pushing me the entire way. She is my everything. Without her I would be nowhere. She made sure I found time to write and worked diligently to minimize distractions. Every time I felt discouraged, she was right there to pick me up. Thank you. I love you.

I have been blessed to have two of the greatest parents anyone can have. My mom and dad never missed a game or a performance. They always pushed me to do and be my best and loved me no matter the outcome. You are either successful because of your family or in spite of it. I can say definitively that my success is owed to the life and love they gave me.

My siblings have always supported me. Jennifer, Daniel, Michael, Cindy, and Katherine, we are as close as any family could be. Thank you for the continued love and support through both the good times and the bad.

Thank you to all the various bosses and unnamed executives I have worked with, both good and bad. You have cemented my management philosophy, and if you were terrible, you provided great material for this book.

Finally, I want to thank the team at Scribe. Without their support and encouragement, this book would not exist. Special thanks to Hal and Emily for leading our weekly calls and keeping us motivated and accountable!

INTRODUCTION

WHY YOU ARE HERE

You are trying to understand madness with logic. This is not unlike searching for darkness with a torch.

—THE MAD HATTER

I walked into the conference room not really knowing what to expect. I sat across the table from someone who had been my boss for two months. Yet he was the one responsible for determining my raise. I listened as he read through my accomplishments for the year. This was the first time he had ever actually seen them. Just like normal, I had to fill in and write my own review because I was not sure anyone actually knew everything I had done. He paused as he noted one blemish. I had missed a project deadline, and that was going to be the reason I didn't get as large of a raise that year. He then proceeded to inform me about the importance of meeting our goals.

It was hard to hold in the disgust I felt. I wondered if he noticed the twisted look on my face. I probably looked like I was holding in a sneeze. I was judged lacking due to someone else's decision. I'd missed that delivery because an executive had set an arbitrary deadline without talking to anyone that actually had to do the work. I had spent eighty-plus hours a week doing everything I could to hit that deadline, but the project date had no basis in fact. Yet I was the one being punished for it. Someone had made a bad decision and I was literally paying the price. Why did no one care to hear the reasons why it was missed? Why was I being judged by someone I had just met? It didn't make any sense.

I left that meeting feeling dejected. What more could I possibly do? How could I win?

These scenarios play themselves out in companies everywhere because, fundamentally, corporate "culture" is broken. My livelihood depended on figuring this out.

You must learn to function in a broken system of stack ranking, layoffs, promotion quotas—the list goes on and on. Without this functional knowledge, you will have a terrible career or, worse, be laid off. The game is survival. Due to this broken culture, middle management is easily one of the toughest jobs in all of existence. It's rough. There is very little support to go around, and the challenges come from all directions. You're often thrown into a job with very little training or explanation of what is expected of you. You must handle difficult employees and difficult bosses.

The harsh truth is that no one cares about your career but you. Former GE CEO Jack Welch famously said, "Take control of your destiny or someone else will." It is a powerful reminder of where you really are. You must take control of this situation or be at the mercy of others, just as I was. You will pay the price for others' blunders. Because of this, you must find a way to navigate the bad decisions you are asked to implement. I am not alone, and neither are you. The fact of the matter is *you are right*: the company *is* full of morons. What's worse? You are actually at the mercy of those morons to put food on the table. There is nothing more frustrating than being held accountable for another's wrong decisions. How do you survive? How do you not let a bad boss or a bad company decision affect your career? We have all faced this situation at one point or another, wondering, *What do I do?*

We are going to face that question head-on in this book. I will walk you through the strategies that you can use to endure the insanity that surrounds you.

Who am I? I am you: another suffering middle manager who has had to learn the hard way the joys and pitfalls of working for a large corporation. I hit all the checkboxes I thought I needed in order to be successful. Got a computer engineering degree and then an MBA. Spent two more years working and getting Six Sigma certified. I thought I knew exactly the path needed to be successful in the corporate world.

My first few years as a manager, I worked trying to figure out how to climb the ladder and do a good job. The more I worked, the more the things around me didn't pass any commonsense standard. I struggled through corporate bureaucracy and policies that made no sense. At one point, I actually considered the possibility I might be going insane.

Slowly, however, patterns began to emerge. I started to notice how others were being successful, and through the guess-and-test method, I came across certain actions that seemed to work in all situations for all bosses. Executives *did* behave within a set of rules, but not rules governed by traditional logic or common sense. I had thought millionaire executives made rational decisions based on hard data and intelligence. I was so naive.

I did well in school, but what I found is that school

doesn't prepare you for the reality of the work world. In school, there is a direct correlation between how hard you work and the grades you receive. If you study for hours and hours, you are probably going to receive an A. This principle does not follow you into the work world. You can put in eighty hours a week and fail. You can put in eighty hours a week and get passed over for a promotion that goes to the person who worked forty hours. There is what feels like an inherent unfairness in the way the system is set up.

The truth is the game *is* inherently biased because it is being judged by humans. It is not a long jump to bitterness and depression when these things occur. The only way to be successful in this biased environment is to know the rules. I have succeeded despite the best efforts of those whose judgment would be considered less than competent.

In the next few chapters, you are going to learn a few things:

- We are going to start with how to stop wasting your energy persuading people they are wrong.
- You'll see that it is difficult to move forward with a bad plan, but counterintuitively, your career depends on doing just that.
- We'll discuss the need to understand what your boss

actually cares about and how to make sure you are solving the problem that matters.

- You will learn to control the narrative so that when everything blows up (as it inevitably will), the finger is not pointing back at you.
- The most powerful lesson in this book we will discuss is that reality does not matter; only perception does. It does not matter if you work eighty hours and someone else works forty. If the perception is the other person is a "hard worker," you are fighting a perception battle, and you need to learn how to control it.

There is truth to the old saying "You can't fix stupid." However, you do have control of how that stupidity affects you and your career.

I decided to write this book because of the lack of support I received throughout my career. I watched as friends were promoted to their first management jobs and had to continually call me for advice. In addition to a lack of support in general, there is a war on middle management. Trying to create a flat organization and removing layers is all the rage. Who doesn't want a utopia where there are no bosses? Google famously tried to do that in 2002. They tried to get rid of all their managers, and what happened? The move ushered in complete chaos. It only lasted a few months before Google realized their mistake and brought the managers back.

What Google found, which should be abundantly clear to you, is that great managers, and more so middle management, are vitally important. Gallup found that managers account for at least 70 percent of the variance in employee engagement scores across business units. In a 2014 report called "State of the American Workplace," Gallup found that only 30 percent of US employees are engaged at work. What does that tell us? Managers are hugely important, and most managers are terrible. I don't believe middle managers are terrible because they are just bad at their jobs. Their terribleness is a by-product of not being supported and having very little control over the decisions that are made. I remember when I was promoted to my first manager position. Did I get extensive training or coaching? Nope. I had a one-day course on how to be a manager. Everything else is on-the-job learning. You are not going to get support from your organization. The only support is going to be from other middle managers.

A couple of caveats. This book will *not* make the people around you smarter, and sadly, it won't even make them easier to endure. What it will do is teach you how to turn others' bad decisions into an opportunity for improvement and potentially even advancement. The concepts in this book, however, will not get you promoted immediately. This is not a "get rich quick" scheme. Climbing the corporate ladder takes time and patience unless you are related to the owner—if that's the case, then, congratulations!

I know what you're thinking: *Time and patience? These are the very last two things anyone wants to have or develop.* It is difficult to remember that your career is a long game. When you are facing frustrating situations, it's easy to get lost in the moment and think this moment will destroy everything. You can't give in to that temptation. As I will explain later, no one will remember those moments but you.

This is not a leadership book. The world doesn't lack a set of plans for how to be a great leader. There are numerous individuals who can tell you how to be an incredible leader, whether they be Steve Jobs, Richard Branson, or Jim Collins. They are CEOs and billionaires and great business minds. None of that is of any help to you today, where you are right now.

I cared deeply about my team and I wanted to be a great leader, so naturally, I read all the leadership books I could find. I tried to absorb everything I could about being a leader. Those books are great, and they are completely worthless to you. The challenge is those books are really focused on more of an executive audience and, honestly, a rosy picture of the world. You can be a great leader and a wonderful person, but as a middle manager, you are going to be stuck with someone who is not. It doesn't matter how great a leader you are if your immediate boss is a clown. You can do everything that Jim Collins tells you to do and still get screwed over. You need to learn to survive in corporate reality.

One of the tenets you read about in those books over and over is how important it is to communicate the "why" of decisions and set a clear vision. Well, that's a great theory, but my boss didn't tell me why we are doing what we are doing. How am I supposed to translate that to my team? "Our executive's have decided to lay off our best people so they can create synergy." Fantastic! I'm looking forward to telling my team all about synergy and our CEO getting a raise. Double my team's workload with no increase in resources? Sure, don't mind if I do!

Sometimes the reasons the decisions were made are wrong, and you don't agree. You are going to think the "why" of a decision is stupid, and yet you have to pick up the pieces and implement them anyway.

I must have missed that chapter in all those leadership books. We are going to focus on that in this book head-on.

Okay, breathe, just breathe. It's all going to be okay.

What you should get from the pages that follow is one

overarching theme: the realization that you are managing people, not projects. How you manage the people around you—from your boss, to your team, to your peers—is ultimately what will determine the course of your career. The results from your projects and initiatives are fleeting and quickly forgotten. Learning to correctly lead and manage the people in your circle of influence is the pathway to successfully executing bad decisions.

And now...on to *the insanity!*

CHAPTER 1

YOU HAVE ALREADY LOST

Of all strategies, knowing when to quit may be the best.
— CHINESE PROVERB

I sat in my gray cubicle twiddling my thumbs, both excited and nervous to meet the new boss. Our company had just gone through a big reorganization, which had changed everything. We were all trying to adjust to a new reality. My previous boss had told me she was leaving and moving on to something bigger and better. It sounded good, but I was sad to see her go and, at the same time, a little excited about the prospect of change. I didn't know much about the new guy, just heard he could be demanding.

The phone started ringing. It was my new director calling to introduce himself. We small-talked for a while and he laid out his expectations for the team. He asked me what my five-year plan was. Then he talked about concrete steps of how he could help me to get there. I was elated! It seemed like he would be someone who could help propel my career to new heights. One of the key points he made was that I needed to work on visibility. He wanted to make sure I was traveling more often to all the different regions we supported. After that call, I grabbed my computer with excitement and started to plan and book the next three months of travel to comply with this new mission. However, two months later, that boss was gone. Another area of the company needed his expertise more.

The phone started ringing; director number three for the year was on the line. He made it clear that the expense budget was tight and all travel needed to be approved in advance by him. All my trips were promptly cancelled. My visibility was cancelled.

Three months later, the phone started ringing. Boss number four let me know a decision had been made that our team needed to move to a different part of the organization, and he was excited to work with me. He went on to say he had evaluated our team and didn't feel we needed to make any changes. I was relieved. Finally, perhaps, I could get some actual work done. Then it was decided my team had dual responsibilities, so I was going to have a "dotted-line" boss as well. Two bosses, two staff meetings. I picked up the phone once again, and my new dotted-line boss number five told me that he had some good ideas for changes that needed to be made.

This insane year came to an end, but I only *thought* the insanity would stop. My end-of-year review started well enough, but my boss was disappointed I hadn't traveled to the regions I supported and wasn't happy with some of our changes. I just stared blankly. I should stop answering the phone.

* * *

Do you remember where you were when you realized you were surrounded by insanity? It could have been a moment such as what I experienced above or something even more insane. The experience is a bit like Alice tumbling down the rabbit hole. Everything you think you know is about to not make any sense. People are not rational, and more importantly, companies are not either.

Once you come to this realization and your worldview is shattered, everything changes. You begin to see the glitches in the system that were always there but that you never noticed before. You begin to second-guess company policies. You start to wonder about the real reason people were promoted. The anonymous employee surveys don't seem so anonymous anymore. Every idea you hear now leads to a time for a pause to understand the motivation behind it. This can really mess with your mind. Your initial reaction when you see this insanity may be that you have to run and tell someone.

It is as if you are the only one who can see what is really going on, and no one will believe it. There is a primal desire that wells up to fight back, to scream at the top of your lungs, "This is a bad idea!" Bad ideas and decisions are flowing left and right, and it feels as if nothing can stop the tide.

What is going on?

Now for the harsh truth: *It's over. You have already lost.*

You may think you can do something about it, but you can't.

YOU CAN'T CHANGE PEOPLE'S MINDS

"We are going to reduce our network capacity by fifteen percent with this project," the executive boldly told the room. His statement radiated confidence. I looked around at the others seated and could not detect even a hint of disagreement. The only problem with his statement was that it was completely untrue. As an engineer, this factual inaccuracy really bothered me, and I could not let it stand unchallenged.

"That's not accurate," I said from my seat at the conference table.

Fifty heads swiveled in my direction, all with the same shocked expression.

The executive coldly stared me down. "Yes, it is."

I proceeded to walk to a whiteboard and explain how our $10 million project would not make any improvement to our network capacity. It was cold, simple math. The executive brushed off my explanation with a wave of his hand.

"You are not correct. It is a fact this will provide millions in savings."

I sat down, dumbfounded at what had just happened. I mathematically proved his statement was false, and yet neither he nor anyone else in the room was swayed. The company spent the $10 million and took a year to complete the project. After the results were seen in the real world, a single email was sent to the planning teams. This email stated that the projections were off and that the potential savings for this project would be less than anticipated. It was never spoken of again.

The very first thing you need to realize is that once people have decided, it is almost impossible to change their minds. A classic 1956 study in the *Journal of Abnormal and Social Psychology* showed that once we decide, we start to like our decision more and to dislike all the other alternatives. Once we form an opinion, we hold on to it and don't let go, despite any evidence to the contrary. We view our decisions through rose-colored glasses and reflectively dismiss anything that does not conform to our new worldview. You are going to attempt to change their mind with facts. This won't work because you are up against motivated reasoning.

What is motivated reasoning, you ask? It is the phenomenon of facts going into our ears and then our brains warping them to conform to fit whatever worldviews we happen to hold. Thinking critically and weighing all the facts in a decision is hard work. Our brain would rather just take a shortcut, dismiss the facts, and work on other, more important things, like what we should watch on TV that night. People believe whatever they want to believe and can use very little evidence to justify their beliefs, even if there is ample evidence to the contrary.

You already know this. Just look at our political landscape.

No matter which side you are on, you find it almost impossible to figure out how those on the other side got their ideas. You are certain they must be complete idiots. Guess what? Your boss is no different. If you can't come around to see their point of view, they probably can't figure out where you got your opinion either. They think that *you* are the moron!

I imagine you want to dismiss this concept because you want to believe that people are rational and that you can persuade them because your argument is just fundamentally right. This is blatantly wrong. Psychologists have known since at least the 1970s that human beings are fundamentally irrational. Your company is not reasonable. There are reasonable individuals within your organization, but taken as a whole, your company is illogical and unreasonable. This is a *fact*. Accept this and you can save yourself a lot of time and frustration.

"But...I have so many brilliant ideas! They will listen to me."

Let's go ahead and put this to bed. No, they won't. No one cares about your brilliance but you.

YOU HAVE NO POWER

Why won't they listen? You also need to fully grasp how

little authority you have. In large organizations, there is a massive power imbalance. Basically, you have none. This is a tough concept to accept and grasp, so I have a feeling you need to see a picture. That one below is the Pyramid of Power! It sounds so cool until you realize it is an upside-down pyramid, and you are at the bottom. You see that little dot at the bottom? That is you. Harsh truth time: you're not that important. Resist and they'll just get another dot. As much as you think you are the cog that keeps everything moving, if you left, they would be fine.

PYRAMID OF POWER

YOU HAVE NO INFLUENCE

Directly related to the amount of power you have in your company is the amount of influence you have. As a manager, your circle of influence just isn't as big as you think it is. The effective influence of a middle manager varies, but in a large corporation, it is very small. As you go up in an organization, the impact of your decisions grows. Most of the bad decisions that you encounter will have been made too far up for you to make a difference. When it comes down to it, others' opinions matter more than yours. Your bosses and their bosses' opinions are actually what moves the needle. Not yours.

This is kind of depressing. I tell you all this not to let you give in to despair and hopelessness but to help you understand the reality of the situation.

CIRCLE OF INFLUENCE

"Face reality as it is, not as it was or as you wish it to be."
—JACK WELCH, FORMER GE CEO

I have said all this, yet you don't want to believe it. (I know you because I am you.) The decision is made, you are dealing with a massive power imbalance, and yet... you are going to attempt to change your boss's mind anyway. You want to fight the good fight. Fine. I get it. You have to try. At least follow a few guidelines so you don't ruin the next few years of your life.

HOW TO DISAGREE WITH THE BOSS

Disagreeing with your boss is easily one of the most precarious situations for a leader. Done wrong, it can derail your career. Done correctly, it can set you up for a solid, candid relationship. Let's set up a few ground rules.

1. NEVER DO IT IN FRONT OF OTHER PEOPLE.

Honestly, it shocks me to even have to write this. For goodness' sake, *never* disagree with your boss in front of other people. I have personally watched this go very wrong.

We were sitting on the conference call of my executive director's staff meeting. A decision had been made that some managers would now report directly to EDs instead of to a director. During the staff meeting, another manager—let's call him "Bill"—said, "I don't understand why we are not being made directors. It doesn't make sense for us to report directly to an ED. This decision doesn't make sense."

Now, Bill was a smart man. He was well respected and had thus far had a great career. He did, however, fail to understand how his speaking up in front of a group would be received. There was a period of silence as we all anxiously waited for our ED to respond. With a slow, measured tone, she replied, "Well, if you think you are supposed to be working for a director, I can make that happen." A cold silence fell across the conference call. Less than two months later, Bill was moved to another group under a director and never heard from again.

Was he really wrong? His statement may have been factually accurate, but he was wrong in the way he presented it. When you question someone in front of a group, you are not only questioning the decision, you are actually questioning the person. That will be taken as an assault on authority instead of a legitimate question about the policy at hand. The correct way: *always do it alone*. Schedule a meeting face-to-face, give them a call, schedule a call—whatever you need to do to get them alone. Make it clear you want to understand the decision, not commit an assault.

2. VALIDATE THEIR POINT OF VIEW.

You don't know everything. (I mean, I know everything, but you probably don't.) The number of bad decisions and dumb projects that you are going to see over the course of your career will blow your mind. On initial inspection, you will be unable to figure out how a rational person could ever come to the conclusion your executive leadership did. However, it is vitally important that you take the time to grab even a thread of why they might have thought this way. If you can't find one, try harder. Take a day. Despite what you think, they did make this decision for a perceived benefit, even if it is wrong. You have to validate that there might even be a reason why they did this. This signals to your leadership that you have thought about the problem and are not having an emotional reaction. When you fail to do this, you are questioning their intelligence and decision-making ability. You are there to fix problems, not cause them.

3. COME IN WITH AN ALTERNATIVE SOLUTION.

One of the things I misunderstood when I was a young manager is that your direct superiors do not want your questions or your problems. They have enough problems of their own. You must come in to the situation with an alternative. I had only been a manager for about a year when I started having issues on a project. I had never faced this situation before, and so, naturally, I reached out for help. I gave my director a call. She patiently waited for me to finish explaining the situation and then asked, "What do you want to do?"

"Uhhhhhhhh..." I had run through this conversation in my head and, in my inexperience, had never anticipated that as her response.

"Well, I am not sure..." I mean the entire point of my call was to get her perspective on the situation.

"Okay, when you figure it out, let me know, and I will support you."

Then the conversation was over. I hung up, realizing this had not really helped me at all. But it did later make me understand that I had been given the job of a manager not only to solve problems but to make my boss's life easier. Don't come with problems; come with solutions.

Let's revisit Bill and put these three points into action.

1. Meet one-on-one
   A. After the announcement, Bill would call the ED *directly* to discuss so there would not be an audience.
2. Validate
   B. He would change the framing: "I can see why we

are making this decision, as it makes sure the EDs have a direct line of communication to the teams and eliminates a layer." He would set the tone: "You guys are so smart; I see what you are trying to do."

3. Offer a solution

C. "Potentially, it makes sense as well for us to have an opportunity to be moved to director roles, as our scope of responsibility is increasing. What do you think?"

This is a significantly less confrontational way to disagree with the big boss. You do it in private, you validate how smart they are, and then you offer an alternative. If Bill had followed these simple rules, he may have never been sidelined.

ONE-REBUTTAL RULE

Another important point to keep in mind is that you get one chance to change someone's mind. One rebuttal. After that, you have got to move on. This is just as important as the three previous ground rules. Construct your argument and make your point, and your leader will immediately let you know that your concerns have been heard. If you do not get immediate agreement, *stop talking immediately*. I have watched my peers make the mistake of continuing to bring up disagreements.

It didn't end well. I have even seen it within my own team when people disagree with my decisions. Nothing is more irritating than setting a direction and having it continually questioned, over and over again. If you do that, enjoy the bottom-of-the-stack ranking. This also applies to "I told you so." If you have already made your point and the decision blows up, do not say anything. Ever. They already know.

You have the ground rules, and now you are going to go disagree with your boss. Go ahead. I will wait...

How did it go? Shocking! It didn't work. The decision is already made. You are not going to be able to change anyone's mind. Even the most persuasive, well-reasoned argument can fail when placed under the wheels of organizational chaos.

What does this all tell us when we put it together? There is but one path we can forge, and that is forward. We have no choice but to move ahead or get left behind. Even knowing this fact, I still had to be taught this lesson over and over again.

Our company decided they needed to save money. One of the ways in which they pursued this was to offshore a portion of our software development. The company's motive was purely financial; they could hire five developers overseas for the price of one in the States. It is hard to argue against that math. I was opposed to this course of action because, through experience, I knew that this had slowed down projects and required a lot of overhead from my team to manage. Overseas developers can be a great resource, but the skillset they could bring to the table was not a good fit for the current project. To put it plainly, it was an inefficient arrangement. I argued heavily against the idea on more than one occasion. I did not agree with the trade-offs the leadership had decided to accept. Since I had such aggressive deadlines, I avoided using offshore labor whenever I could. Since the individuals who make these decisions were not on the front lines, they did not actively see the additional challenges and roadblocks this arrangement creates for the development manager and local teams.

I was feeling pretty good toward the end of the year after I'd managed to hit all of the objectives that the company had laid out. Well, at least I *thought* I had. However, I soon learned that I had been labeled as a "resister" to offshore labor, which had put me at odds with senior leadership. Even though I was correct, I received negative feedback. "You did a great job, but I can't give you a higher rating because you resisted working with our offshore teams."

It was at that point when I began to realize the futility

of the entire process. I would have to figure out how to execute decisions I did not agree with, or my career was going to be in trouble.

To be successful, you have no choice but to learn how to execute decisions you don't agree with. Is a decision actually right or wrong? Decisions are just trade-offs, and sometimes you will not agree with those trade-offs. Your boss may choose to reduce quality for money or lay off good people to make shareholders happy. It doesn't matter whether they are right or wrong. What matters is that they are in charge. In this role, you are a follower. Your career is at the mercy of other people. Get on the train and move forward. Throughout the rest of this book, I will take you through how to do that so you can protect your career and survive the chaos.

KEY TAKEAWAYS

1. It is almost impossible to change someone's mind after a decision has been made.

2. You do not currently have enough power and influence to affect most decisions.

3. Disagree with your boss the right way.

   • Talk with them one-on-one.

   • Validate their point of view.

   • Present an alternative solution.

4. *One* rebuttal. You only get one shot. Take it and move on.

ACTION TO TAKE TODAY

Don't be the hero. Stop worrying about fighting insanity, and figure out the right way to survive bad decisions.

CHAPTER 2

MANAGE YOUR BOSS

*First law of Bad Management: If something
isn't working, do more of it.*

—Tom DeMarco

I walked out of our agile/scrum/DevOps/ [insert your
own buzzword here] training with a new perspective on
things. I honestly was looking forward to our company
embracing a faster way of developing projects and processes. It almost seemed too good to be true!

They drilled into us the idea that we needed to move fast
and "be agile"—no need to understand a few years' worth
of projects. We needed to focus only on the next three
months and not be stuck to a regimented plan because by
the time month twelve rolled around, our plans would be
so out of date they'd be laughable. This desire to preplan

everything had meant we were caught in an endless cycle of being behind what the business actually needed. For the first time in a long time, I felt a tiny glimmer of hope in my soul, a slightly warm feeling that I might be able to make it another day, that there were a few competent people around here after all.

A mere one week later, I found an email waiting for me. My planning manager was asking for a list of all of our projects and deliverables for the next twelve months, with business cases; otherwise, we would not receive a budget. "Agile" thinking had lasted a grand total of seven days.

Working for another human being is terrible, simply for the fact that they are another human being. They can be irrational, illogical, and prone to terrible ideas. The worst part of it is that they hold the key to your success. How hard you work or how great your results are don't matter that much if your boss doesn't like you. We would all love to be objectively judged by our competence. That is just not possible.

Good news! All hope is not lost. Just as important as implementing these bad decisions is learning the correct way to manage your boss. In this chapter, we are going to focus on how to do just that, with the least amount of collateral damage, as you execute someone else's bad ideas.

MOTIVATION

To manage your boss effectively, you need to understand their most basic motivations. The truth is that your boss is a very simple person. Your boss only cares about one thing: themselves. You know this instinctively, but we like the concept of our boss caring about us and our career. That's a great thought, and there are some good bosses out there, but when it comes down to it, the boss is there to get paid, just as you are, so they will always protect themselves over you. As Joseph Murphy wrote in *The Power of Your Subconscious Mind* a half-century ago, "The instinct of self-preservation is the first law of nature; your strongest instinct is the most potent of all."

Self-preservation is human nature; nothing wrong with that. The people on your team want to look good to you, your boss wants to look good to their boss, and so on. It is a never-ending hierarchy of everyone trying to impress the person above them, because their paycheck depends on that. In order to understand your boss, you must understand their primary motivation: self-preservation. They may be nice and friendly and "care" about you, but I promise that if they are told to fire you, they will do it in a second. Don't overestimate your value to the company or to your boss.

Now that we know our boss's primary motivation, what do we do with that? Your boss cares about how they look to their boss. So find out what they are measured on. How do you know what your boss's goals are? You ask for them. What does their boss want from them? Countless times, I've seen a mismatch in motivations lead to a surprise.

For some reason, bosses can be a bit cryptic with this information. One of the ways to get around this is to list all of the current things you are working on. Then set up a meeting to review them. The purpose of this meeting is to let your boss prioritize everything you and your team are working on. "Here is a list of everything I have currently. Where do you feel I should be focusing the majority of my time?" This meeting is not for you to talk; you are there to listen. In doing so, you will uncover exactly which project or task your boss really cares about. I have had multiple major projects I was working on concurrently, but only one of them was actually in my performance agreement for the year. I remember distinctly asking my boss this exact question, and he picked other projects for me to work on! Had I not had that conversation, I would have made the wrong assumption about which one mattered the most. Understanding expectations is a huge part of making everyone around you successful.

We had a new directive come down that we needed to combine multiple teams into one. This new team was going to fall under me. I was going to go from managing eight people to managing nineteen. My scope of responsibility and workload was going to triple. Thankfully, it came with a promotion and a pay raise. *Ha! Just kidding.*

I called up my director and let him know that this was going to be a challenge to handle that many people and still deliver on our projects with the quality expected. I barely got the words out of my mouth before he said, "Well, this is just the nature of the business, and you should make the best of it." I was candid about the issues this new team would face, but where I went wrong was in going immediately to my opinion instead of seeking out his opinion first.

Realizing my error, I had the opportunity to chat with him again a week or two later. I asked him what opportunities he saw for this new large team. He immediately started launching into the fact that with a bigger team, we could take on bigger and more ambitious projects. *Bingo.* That was the right question. The boss wanted to get noticed through my team. Even though it was done for "efficiency," the real problem my boss wanted me to solve was his own visibility. He didn't care about saving money. He wanted something big and flashy. This is a great illustration of how the stated motive for a change and what your boss actually wants may be two completely separate things. You need to understand your boss's goals and expectations. You need to ask vague, leading questions. People love to give their opinion, so give your boss an opportunity to share. Ask:

1. What opportunities do you see with this change?
2. What do you see as the primary benefit of this?
3. I think we could see some value from this. What do you think?

The answers to these questions will be a fantastic indicator of the expectations your boss has for this project/decision. Using this information, you can then determine how to proceed.

Your boss is frustrating. Sometimes it can feel like they are an enigma inside of a fortune cookie. You are doing everything that your boss asks of you and yet, somehow, they still are not happy. It doesn't make any sense! Once again, they are being human and expecting you to somehow telepathically understand what they need.

I had this exact experience during one of my projects that I had thought was going well. I had been asked to audit a process, apply my Six Sigma training, and squeeze a few hours out of the engineer's day. It turned out to be a challenging project, but I was finally able to hit the targets the company was after. However, I received poor feedback from my leader. Right when I was about to throw my hands up in despair, an email was forwarded to me accidentally. This email showed my boss throwing me under the bus for the project and blaming me for not hitting targets soon enough. What was he talking about? I did everything I was asked! Turns out *he* was getting pressure because all of the projects under his team were taking too long to complete. There was an unspoken requirement to finish a six-month project in four months. I had solved the problem I was asked to but had missed the bigger picture of what really mattered: my boss's problem. His problem was the heat he was taking for projects taking too long.

Now, was it his fault for not communicating that with me? Absolutely, but I was still going to get blamed. You have to be proactive in finding out the pain points with your boss. Ask and you shall receive.

We might as well go ahead and stop right here, because that's it. Your path to success runs directly through one individual, and that is your boss. Your goal is to understand what your boss's true challenges are and how to address them.

I should note there is a *huge* difference between making your boss happy and making them successful. To make someone happy is really easy. Just say yes to everything and flatter them endlessly. While it is true you can garner some success this way, it will ultimately end in failure, due to the resentment of those around you, and you will, at some point, be discovered as a yes-man. I am sure you have heard the saying that a rising tide lifts all boats. Well, your boss is the tide. No matter how little you may think of your boss, the job you are in is to make them look good.

SPEAK TRUTH

To make your boss successful, you have to speak open and candidly. When a decision is made that you believe to be bad, you usually think this because of information asymmetry. Either you know something your boss doesn't, or they know something you don't. You have an obligation to make sure your superior is adequately informed of everything you know. The challenge is to make sure your candor does not come across as a challenge to their authority. It's important to note that this candor does not mean you point out everything that is stupid in your company, because there is not enough time in the day for that. No, your candor is to prevent your boss from doing something stupid. You protect your career by protecting theirs.

The key to coming across correctly is to understand your boss's position. Make sure to feel out their perspective of this action *before* you give your opinion. Most of the time, you will not know the origin point of a bad decision and who voted for what. So be careful since your boss may be supportive of whatever insanity is going on.

Let's try a real-life exchange:

Boss: "It has been decided that every employee will have to enter time sheets every week, even if they are salaried."

Me: (*Internal voice: what a giant pain, everyone on my team is going to hate this.*) "Okay, I can see why that makes sense from a business perspective. What do you think will be the primary benefit of this new policy (*which is stupid*)?"

Boss: "Well, I am not sure. I think they just want to track who is working on what project."

We just got two *huge* pieces of information in that sentence; the boss doesn't really know what is going on either, and he didn't think of it or support it.

Me: "This is going to be very unpopular, and a huge challenge every week to track every single meeting we attend and for what purpose. Seems like a lot of overhead."

Boss: "Yeah, I agree, but I think we just have to suck it up and do it."

This conversation actually happened, and we learned a lot. The boss isn't really on board but has to do it. I was candid with my objections, but as we talked about in Chapter 1, the decision was over; no need to push any further. My objections were stated; time to get on with it.

Let's review:

1. Make sure you get your boss's opinion on the situation *first*.
2. *Then* be candid if they were not the originator of the policy or if you are explicitly asked for feedback.
3. Move on.

What should you do if your boss is the one who comes up with the terrible idea? This situation gets a little bit trickier.

Boss: "It has been decided that every employee will have to enter time sheets every week, even if they are salaried."

Me: "Okay, I can see why that makes sense from a business perspective. What do you think will be the primary benefit of this new policy (which is stupid)?"

Boss: "This is going to be a great new way for us to track who is working on what project. This information is going to help us figure out staffing in the future."

Me: "This might create some additional overhead for our teams. I think there is potential of some hesitation to do this."

You will note that I softened my criticism, as my boss's stance is not as clear. However, I did not hold back on being candid.

Boss: "Really? I think the teams will see the value..."

The key to everything is to do your best to understand your boss's position before you open your mouth. Even when you have an opposing viewpoint, make sure to be candid with your feedback. Being candid is not the same thing as being harsh. You can word your feedback in a way that gets your point across without it being taken the wrong way. This feedback follows the one-rebuttal rule from the earlier chapter. Your boss only needs your opinion one time. After that, move on.

MAKE THEIR LIFE BETTER

We all wish that we were the boss, and we all think we could do it better. As much as your boss's life looks amazing and easy, we have a tendency to underestimate the bad days they can have and the amount of pressure they could be under. We exist to take some of that pressure off. We do that by ensuring we are solving their actual problem and sharing some of the burden. You can do that with one simple question: "I know you have a lot going on—is there anything I can help you out with this week?"

This simple phrase can transform your relationship. Your intention is to be viewed as someone who is trying to help solve their problems. This different perception can make a world of difference. Try to ask this question only twice in a month. Don't overuse it because it becomes meaningless; you don't want to pester them. It is true that there are some pitfalls to putting yourself out there. Your boss could potentially overwork you or take advantage of you. The potential benefits outweigh the potential for abuse. Just know that whoever this is will not be your boss for the next ten years. Endure it. It is just a tiny speck of time in your overall career. You are building for the long term.

ASK THEM FOR ADVICE

You need to make your boss invested in your career, to feel like they will be a part of your success. You do this by asking them for advice. Alison Wood Brooks of Harvard Business School talks about how we have it wrong about asking for advice. We worry that people won't think we are competent if we have to ask for help, but actually, the opposite is true. "This is because being asked for advice is flattering, it feels good," Wood said in a 2016 article.

"They're asking for my advice because they think I'm smart and I know the answer, and I think they're smart because I'm actually going to tell them things that will be useful and help them do the task better."

You know who likes to feel smart? Everyone. Especially your boss; they like to be thought of as a great leader. You don't want to misuse this interaction, but strategically placed questions will allow your boss to feel a part of your success. Then they will be happy if you do well because they'll feel like it reflects on their amazing leadership. Some great questions you can ask include "I have learned so much in this job—what do you feel I should focus on next?" Or how about "There are some great opportunities in the company right now with all this growth—what do you think is the next big opportunity for us?" You give them a chance to talk about how smart they are, and if you act on any of their advice, they get to feel like they directed it and are the cause. It is a win-win scenario for both of you. Don't be afraid to ask them for career advice.

WHY DOES YOUR TEAM EXIST?

Your team exists to solve a problem. What is that specific problem? The only way to be effective is to understand the value your team brings not only to the company but also to your boss. In one of my previous roles, I led a team of project managers. The purpose of that team was to coordinate large projects between departments and make sure executives always had the most current status. That team solved the problem of coordination and information. You need to pinpoint and identify the exact problem *your* team solves, so you can make sure you are solving that.

My team had just been given a huge new software application to build. It was imperative that we get the end user feedback and build something that would save them time and effort. In a project like this, there are usually multiple goals. Number one is to deliver a great product that people are happy with. But talking with my boss, I understood that there was another point to this project. They were trying to change the perspective of our organization, to show we can move fast and communicate better. It would have been easy to miss this secondary objective had I not been in close communication with my boss. This goal was not explicitly stated but was easily inferred through conversations. Even if I had delivered a great product, had I not also moved at a fast pace, my team would have been considered a failure. The only way to get this information was through discussion with my boss.

PROTECT YOUR BOSS

You know this decision is going to go south at some point.

Either it is your boss's fault or the fault of someone above them. Remember how we talked about self-preservation being human beings' (and your boss's) primary motivation? You not only have to protect yourself from the fallout, but you have to shield your boss as much as you can too.

Do you think anyone gets very far pointing the finger at their boss? Nope. Why would I want to hire someone who just made their previous boss look bad? How long would it be until they did the same to me? It is important to keep as many of the variables pointing away from your boss as you can. When you build the lessons learned, make sure nothing directly references the fact that they were directly responsible. Instead, ensure that the causes or obstacles are due to "unforeseen" or "unavoidable" issues.

Let's run through an example:

"The project is in jeopardy due to resource constraints."

The real story is that your boss planned horribly.

"The deliverables for this project turned out to be larger than anticipated."

The boss overworked everyone.

The key is to point out the issue without directly pointing out the party who is responsible. This can be irritating, but suck it up. If you protect your boss, they are more apt to protect you. At some point, you will make a bad decision, and the failure will be your fault. You are hoping to get reciprocity when you make a mistake. Never throw your boss to the wolves; it will only backfire.

Why do we have to do all this? Because you need grace for the inevitable mistake. You are trying to execute a terrible decision that will not reflect well on you. If the boss likes you and you make their life easier, they will cut you some slack, and this will merely be a bump in the road. Star players get better treatment.

Jimmy Johnson, the former head coach of the Dallas Cowboys, talks about how a player once fell asleep during the team meeting. He proceeded to make an example of this player by screaming at him and kicking him out of the meeting.

Someone asked him, "What would you have done if it had been Troy Aikman, your star quarterback?"

He responded, "I would have walked over and said, 'Hey Troy, wake up.'"

Follow these keys and you get to be Troy Aikman.

DOES YOUR BOSS ACTUALLY MATTER?

You have now read an entire chapter on how to manage your boss, but let's back up. Does your boss actually matter? Do you have to make your boss successful in order for you to be a success? Short answer: no. But the more complicated answer is that it will be much easier to be promoted and be successful if your boss is on your side.

When I was an engineer, we were acquired by another company. This transition was not easy, to say the least. The workload doubled, and everyone was miserable. I knew I had to find a way out. So I applied for a new internal manager position. The way the HR system worked, my immediate manager got an email letting them know I had applied for another position. As I drove home that evening, my phone rang; it was my boss. "I see that you have applied for another job," he said. "How you perform in your current job is what determines whether you will have any opportunities in the future, and right now, you are not performing at a high enough level."

I was working fifty hours, but the workload was closer to sixty to seventy hours a week. I couldn't keep up, so on that point, he was correct. One month later, I was promoted to manager of a new team. I walked into his office to let him know I had accepted the promotion. The hiring director never even called to get his opinion. Why? Because I had built allies. (We will talk about how to do that in future chapters.)

I had gone to another manager that I respected and had worked with in the past and asked him to reach out to the hiring director on my behalf. This got my foot in the door, and I did the rest.

Is it possible to succeed without your boss being behind you? Yes, but it is the exception rather than the rule.

I have seen the opposite happen as well. When I was hiring for an open position on my team, I had another manager tell me that one of my candidates could be "high maintenance." Do you think I wanted to deal with that? Nope. I passed on him and went to the next one on the list. Your most direct path to success will lead through your current boss. Focus on that relationship extensively and you will be better off.

* * *

I conclude this chapter with one slight exception to boss patterns: the tyrant. There is such a thing as a truly awful human being, someone you cannot make happy or successful. Over my career, I have worked with a lot of bosses. Some good and some bad, but for a short time, I had to report directly to a boss that fit the definition of every horrible boss you have heard of. He stands out as the worst.

He was a high-level executive who walked around with an air of arrogance. He wore ties to work, even though the dress code was casual. Micromanager? Yes. Two-faced? Yes. Placed all blame at others' feet? Yes.

I remember creating a PowerPoint deck he wanted for my project. He didn't like it. We spent three grueling hours on a conference call, poring over every inch of the slide deck. *Font sizes. Colors. Backgrounds.* Yes, we spent an hour on font size, and he couldn't just do it and send back his edits. No, he wanted to make suggestions and watch me do it.

We reached one slide where he let out a verbal sound of disgust, "Ugh, I really do not like that sentence right there."

I worked hard to hide my laughter. "That was your sentence," I said. "I copied and pasted that directly from what you sent me."

"Oh, okay, well, let's move to the next one, then."

I wrote a lot in this chapter about how to interact with your boss, find their challenges, and help them succeed. The truth is, some bosses are just jerks, and nothing you do is going to work. This guy was impossible.

However, there is hope. They will not be your boss for your entire career, and just as with horrible decisions, there are things you can do to mitigate the damage. I let out a sigh of relief when, several years later, the company let him go.

The most important person in your life is not your spouse or significant other. It is your boss. The truth is, you are going to spend more time at work than at home. You had better have a good relationship with your boss, or the frustration will leak into other areas of your life. Make the boss your ally through doing what we discussed above. When it comes down to it, your boss is a simple person and wants the same thing everyone else wants: to protect their job. Keep your focus on making them successful and solving the problems that your team is intended to solve. If you make their life better, they will, in turn, not make your life as awful. This is not an overnight solution, as building this type of relationship will take time. However, if you lay the foundation, not only will your boss be successful, but you will be too.

KEY TAKEAWAYS

1. Your boss is a simple person and will always protect themselves and their career first.

2. Build a relationship by being truthful and candid.

3. Focus on making their life better and solving their actual problems.

4. Always protect them.

5. Don't be afraid to ask them for advice and get them invested in you and your career.

ACTION TO TAKE TODAY

Call your boss and ask them, "I know you have a lot on your plate right now—is there anything that I can help with?"

CHAPTER 3

FIND THE CRACKS

Problems in a company are like cockroaches in the kitchen. You will never find just one.

—WARREN BUFFETT

I was driving down the interstate, and I heard a loud *CRACK*. The sound was deafening and caused me to jump. I looked across my windshield and found that I was now the proud owner of a small rock chip. It was actually quite surprising that such a loud sound came from such a small crack.

I didn't think much of it, but a week later, I noticed that it had grown slightly, with various hairline cracks sprouting in all sorts of wonderful directions. Like most good motorists, I chose to ignore it, and before long, those cracks covered my entire windshield, which had to be replaced.

One of the unintended consequences of terrible decisions is they actually create *more* problems than they solve. A bad decision is exactly like that rock chip—it starts small, then grows and spreads problems in all different directions. This is terrible for the company but *great* for you personally. You have a job not because you are a genius or you are amazing. No, they keep you employed because you solve a problem. The key to keeping that employment is to look for other ways you can add value. This is a vitally important step for protecting yourself. The more problems you can solve, the more valuable you are for the organization. The company creates a steady stream of problems for you to fix. If you can be the one not only to identify those new problems but also to have a realistic suggestion on how to fix them, your career is going to move in the right direction.

THE YEARLY RAISE

We all sit through our performance reviews, waiting for our raise, this magical number to be revealed. Traditionally, a target number was set, and then managers could move that a few percentage points in either direction based on performance for the year. Pay was based on performance. Makes sense, right? As a manager, I had the ability to give my top performers just a little extra as a thank-you for their hard work.

Notice how I said it makes sense? Remember how I also said that your company is not rational? Our company decided this system wasn't "fair." Instead, yearly raises would now be determined by a computer formula. It would consider years of service, current pay, and geographic location. The computer would spit out a number that was set in stone and could not be modified. Managers had no input.

The result of this bad idea was that some high performers, the best people in the company, would get 1 percent or even 0 percent raises. The computer decided they were paid too much. When inflation is considered, the company had effectively decided to pay our best people less each year. Oh, did I mention that low performers could end up with 6 percent or more, because a computer said they were not paid enough? This one change effectively eliminated a pay-for-performance culture. What could go wrong?

I was not immune to this either. My boss was nice enough to tell me that, based on my performance, he would have given me a bigger raise, but he couldn't because the computer wouldn't let him. That really helped my motivation the next year! All of the managers naturally argued against this change, but their voices fell on deaf ears. HR wanted to remove any bias from the system, and as a little bonus, they got to pay people a little less.

They didn't trust the managers' judgment in these complicated matters of rating people anymore.

The decision to change the pay structure effectively upended the culture in the entire organization. As a middle manager, I was left holding the bag and trying to hold the pieces together. The change had fractured our windshield. What was I going to do? How was I going to keep my team focused?

I found an answer. Although the people who created the policy had not intended this, they had given me a bad guy to work against. I could say, "I agree you deserve a raise, but the new rating system does not allow it." I actually was able to remove a potential point of contention between the manager and the team! Managers were no longer the ones standing between people and their paycheck. We were on their side!

This new reality was not unlike the experience of a new car purchase. The salesman and I will engage in an epic battle over the price of the vehicle. I will make an offer and he will say, "Oh, not sure if we can do that, let me go see what I can do." He will walk over to this elevated desk where all the managers sit and make a grand display of working for us. Then he'll come back, saying he finally got "them" to agree. Why do they do this? It is so the salesman is not seen as the bad guy; the salesman is your friend! He is working for you! See how hard he works? It is the evil dealership that won't agree to your price.

So there actually was a good unintended benefit to this bad idea. It made a manager's job easier and harder at the same time. It was harder because I couldn't reward my best team members. However, the manager was no longer the bad guy at the end of the year. That mantle had shifted to the company. They will hate the company, but they can still love you. I am sure you have undoubtedly heard that people leave bad bosses, not bad jobs. Now I had one less reason for them to hate me, so that was something.

I say this not to tell you to "always be positive and focus on the bright side," because that is just unrealistic. Sometimes there are bad decisions you just have to deal with. You can, however, figure out a way to use the effects of those bad decisions to help yourself and better your team.

This new pay policy left a crack in our company culture. We no longer had a concrete way to recognize our top performers the way they expected. That's a problem. To solve this problem that the company had created, we had to create new ways to keep our employees engaged and feeling valued. I made sure, for my best people, that I was as flexible with requests for work-from-home days and other perks I had control of, but it wasn't enough. We also had an internal system that let us give small monetary awards, usually under one hundred dollars, as a thank-you to employees, with director approval. I talked with my director about the issues the pay-raise policy would cause and let him know I planned to make more use of that system to ensure my best people understood their hard work would not go unnoticed. You would be surprised how much even people with six-figure salaries appreciate a fifty-dollar gift card. My handing these out throughout the year to show appreciation made a big difference.

Maybe this new pay policy did solve bias with some of the terrible managers, but it also created a lot of cracks in the culture. Find the issues and solve them.

FOCUS ON THE PEOPLE

I learned the value of building relationships on bad projects during my time working on Six Sigma process improvements. One of the projects assigned to me was just bad. I won't go into detail, as you would fall asleep, but needless to say, there was no way it was going to be successful. Among the challenges, I had to cold-call directors for information and get them on board with what I was doing.

Four years later, I was sitting in an interview with a

director for a new job opportunity. "I remember you when you called me for the Six Sigma project," he said. I had actually forgotten! It was such a brief interaction that my memory had filed it away, but it turned out to be pretty important!

Whom you interact with on a project, good or bad, or as the result of a decision, good or bad, is the most important thing to identify. You are slowly expanding your network and circle of influence through the people you come into contact with. Once you understand who is impacted by a decision, figure out how you can help them. My first interaction with a future boss had turned out to be a cold call on a bad project.

Understand the scope of the bad decision and figure out whom it impacts. My previous example about mandatory time-reporting impacted everyone, so that is easy. Let's look at another controversial decision: outsourcing. This is understandably a sensitive topic for a lot of people. An edict was put down that my team had to use outsourced labor for a project. This decision naturally made the existing team very nervous. It impacted our team directly, but upon further inspection, I saw it had a ripple effect on other teams as well. They were watching to see how successful our project was and the effects it would have. There was potential for this one decision to proliferate throughout the organization.

You need to fully understand the scope of effects of a decision before you can figure out how best to execute on it. Sometimes it takes a while to understand all the ripples. The problem is not as important as the people you will come into contact with. Focus on the people impacted, not whether you believe the decision is good or bad.

UNDERSTAND THE REAL PROBLEM

My wife dug her elbow into my ribs. "You're snoring again," she said. Apparently, she had finally decided that if she didn't get to sleep, then no one did. "We have got to stop your snoring."

What was my wife's problem? The obvious answer was my snoring. But that would be wrong. Her actual problem was she wanted a good night's sleep and wasn't getting it. There were other options besides stopping my snoring that would have achieved her actual goal: a good pair of ear plugs, sleeping in another room, etc.

Just like us, companies tend to get tunnel vision when faced with a problem. They go about solving symptoms instead of the root problem. Be smarter. Look for the root problem and find alternative solutions for that. Most of the people you run across will not be wired to look for the real problem. Your peers are going to get frustrated with the company's problems; keep your head down and move on. You can stand out by finding the real problems and solving those.

Why did the company make this or that decision? You might drive yourself crazy trying to figure this out because the answer may not follow a logical path. The simple answer in most cases: it made someone's life easier.

Let's go through a few examples.

1. There's a new expense policy that makes traveling a nightmare for everyone.
    a. The CFO was told to cut costs, so now his boss will leave him alone.
2. Ten percent of the company is laid off.
    a. A new leader is brought in to "shake things up," so now the board is off his back, and he has bought some time.
3. Your boss asks you for a hard deadline for a project you have no chance of making.
    a. He is told to drive for results, and now he can point to you as the single point of failure instead of himself, which gets his boss off his back.

Almost every decision can be traced back to the desire to please the boss. Everyone has a boss, even the CEO.

They are trying to impress them and keep their jobs. Understand this pain point to know what they are trying to address. Does it actually matter why they made the decision? Not really, because you can't do anything about it anyway. Focus everything you have on trying to understand the *real* problem they want to solve.

You do this through investigation. Talk to every single person in your circle individually and listen for their understanding of the issues.

Get a notebook. I know this is an antiquated idea in a digital society, but putting pen to paper is better for your brain. Every day, write down a problem that you encounter or a frustration that you see in your company. Do this exercise for two weeks straight. You should have, at a minimum, ten things on your list. If your company is anything like the rest, you will have twenty-plus.

At the end of those two weeks, take that list and start to determine potential solutions for each of those problems. This is important: *the solutions do not have to be realistic.* This exercise is just to look at possibilities. Don't try to solve them all in a day. Do this over the course of the next week. Then throw out all those you cannot influence. Your company has so many problems, I guarantee you there will be at least one item on that list you can attack. That's the one.

Go after it with everything you have. Find the solution to the real problem. Don't worry about the list of twenty; narrow your scope to a single issue within your company. Problem solvers keep their job, and the ones who solve problems they were not asked to solve get promoted. Almost every single person tries to "stay in their lane." They do what their job description says, and that is it. If I had a nickel for every time someone said, "Well, that is some other group's problem," I would already be retired and living on an island. You can set yourself apart by taking the problems others have caused and fixing them.

REVEALED UNDER PRESSURE

You will learn more about your company and its people from the failures than from the successes. Do they panic? Do they hold calls all day long? How does your boss react to failure? Did they even admit failure? You know this will fail, so how do they handle it?

They say that true character is revealed under pressure. Nowhere is this truer than in a stressful work situation. Your very livelihood can be threatened by a bad decision. Your bonus, your raise, your life can be overturned due to situations seemingly out of your control. It is enough to raise anyone's stress level. This is a valuable gift if you learn to observe the impact of this stress on those around you. The only way to know who you can count on is to watch how people perform under pressure. The only way to learn to trust your boss is not by seeing how they are when times are good but how things are handled when pressure is coming from all sides.

> "True character is revealed in the choices a human being makes under pressure—the greater the pressure, the deeper the revelation, the truer the choice to the character's essential nature."
>
> —ROBERT MCKEE

I remember playing a football game in which things were not going particularly well. One of our better players came over to the sidelines, sat on the ground, and started to pout like a two-year-old. Before the game, he had been jumping around, yelling, and leading the team onto the field—doing all the right things. Is that someone you want to build your team around? Stress reveals character. People stop pretending who they are under stress.

The only way to know the true makeup of your team is to watch them operate in less-than-ideal situations. The moment the pressure heated up, that player crumpled. This bad decision and all the ones that come after it will tell you who your team truly is, whom you can rely on. Whom you can build around. It will reveal who you are as well! How you react to this situation will determine what others perceive in you. How you behave in an unwinnable scenario will determine if your boss will build a team around you.

In order to be successful and to keep your sanity, you need to find the value in the dumb stuff you are going to be asked to do. The first challenge is to understand the scope of all the people impacted. You can use that to build new relationships and potential allies for the future.

Take a look at all the places this decision touches. What did it break? When you identify this, you have a great opportunity to solve those problems before anyone else sees them.

Finally, use this opportunity as a learning experience to see who you can rely on, on your team and in your peer group. When the pressure is turned up, you are going to have a great opportunity to see whom to rely on in the future. There is opportunity in every activity. As frustrating as it can be to be on the end of those bad decisions, you can turn them around and use them to advance your career.

Next time something stupid comes down, start looking for all the additional problems that it creates and be the one to solve them. *New org structure creating silos?* Set up meetings to break them. *New open offices making every-one work from home?* Schedule a lunch to get everyone together. *Seeing redundant teams?* Make a proposal to bring them all together under you! The biggest marker of a truly bad decision is that it will create more problems than it solves. This will be a huge opportunity for you!

Understand that a bad decision can be a good thing for you and view it through that lens. People really only care if you can make their life better. Can you help them in some way? Do it. As hard as it is to comprehend in the moment, bad decisions are some of the best things that can happen in your career.

KEY TAKEAWAYS

1. Look for all the new problems this bad decision causes.
2. Focus on the people impacted and how you can potentially help them.
3. Don't sit back, waiting for it to be your job; be proactive about attacking issues you can control.
4. Focus on finding the real problem and not the symptom.
5. Watch how people behave under stress. It will tell you whom you can rely on.

ACTION TO TAKE TODAY

Get your notebook out and start documenting the problems you come across.

CHAPTER 4

MANAGE YOUR TEAM

*I'm in the unfortunate position of having
to consider other people's feelings.*

—JERRY SEINFELD

We were all called together for an impromptu company meeting. The new CTO strolled onto the stage in his tailored suit and slicked-back hair. He confidently proclaimed, "I have *exciting news!*" It was hard for him to contain his enthusiasm. "We are reorganizing the company in a way that is going to better align us for the future, buzzword, buzzword, synergies!"

He talked about how this news would require us to streamline our workforce! That was so *exciting*!

Everyone started looking around at each other; we all

knew what that meant. "Guys, this is an exciting moment in our history—*be excited!*"

The blank stares from the crowd did not really reflect the enthusiasm he was going for. Several times, he paused, actually expecting us to applaud. He spoke with the confidence of someone who can make decisions for other people and not be affected. It was one of the most out-of-touch moments I have ever witnessed.

Perhaps in that moment, it was exciting for him, but he never stopped to think about the impact on people or their day-to-day lives. Very shortly, 10 percent of the company was laid off. Morale was low, and productivity was even lower. Most of us walked into our next team meeting with heads hanging. Our leadership began talking about how ambitious our fourth-quarter goals were and how we needed to "do better."

A hand went up tentatively, and the question on everyone's mind finally came out. "We just lost a huge part of our workforce, and the morale is low—this is going to make these goals tough to achieve."

The leadership response was even more telling than the CTO's original announcement. "If morale is low, that is up to you to fix. You need to make sure your team is focused and we hit our goals."

What? This should shock no one, but they didn't even acknowledge that morale was a huge problem. They created this massive issue, and now it was up to the middle managers to somehow fix it! Do you think any of us felt excited? The volume of the work didn't change, yet we now had 10 percent fewer people to do it.

Generating fake excitement cannot overcome the reality of bad decisions. How you deliver the message of a decision can ultimately be one of the drivers of its success or failure. The battle is over; time to implement. What is the right way to communicate a bad idea to your team so you don't lose credibility? How do you ask people to do something you don't believe in?

Before you deliver the company line to your team on why a bad decision was made, remember one key thing: they don't care. What they do care about is how this change will affect them. The question you need to answer is, how will this decision impact your team daily? I see this mistake made over and over again with internal company communication. Most communications stress how great it will be for the company. That's the wrong message. Your audience is not "the company"; it is individuals that happen to work for that company. You have to learn how to craft a message directed at the individuals within the company.

A bad leader would have walked in and reread the company email:

> We must hypergrowth our prospects through finding efficiencies in the size and scope of our team to leverage an innovative agile operating model to ensure our future.

What is this gibberish? What does it even mean? I think leaders have some sort of management thesaurus and feel they need to hit a certain word count. It is a giant waste of time and resources. Think about how long someone spent writing that sentence. I bet it was proofread ten times, and I can picture the guy pushing back from his desk in self-satisfaction. "Man, that is a great sentence. I did good today."

Your entire team reads that crap, and guess who needs to pick up the pieces? That's right, the middle manager. The awful example above is great to reference when it comes time for you to talk with your team. One of the primary jobs of a manager is to translate the gunk that comes down from above into something your team can understand. How does it impact them? Be open, honest, and candid. Let them know your expectations for what will change, even if you are not sure. Much like the scenario above, one of the most difficult situations to go into is after a layoff in which you lose part of the team. I vividly remember my staff meeting right after I had to let someone go. Everyone was staring at the floor; I could sense the concern and shock in the way they carried themselves. They all sat there wondering, *What next? Am I next?*

"As you know," I said, "we had to let go of someone today, and it sucks. It is a bad situation all around, but it is one that we had no choice but to make. Every team in the company got hit, and we were no exception. It is going to be challenging in the interim, but we are going to get through it. Everyone is going to have to help pick up some of that workload. Here is how we are going to divvy up the work going forward...What questions do you have for me? I will do my best to answer them."

That is open and honest communication. Tell them the situation plainly, then tell them a path forward, and most importantly, ask for their input. Give them an opportunity to be heard. They are not dumb; they know that nothing is going to change, but they need to feel that you hear them and that you value their opinion. Your team is probably smarter than you anyway. You need to get their viewpoint as a group or one-on-one. Their perspectives may open up new avenues you did not consider.

TRUST

The most important thing when leading a team is trust.

Does your team trust you to tell them the truth? Does your team trust you to take their best interests into consideration? Trust is hard to gain but very easily lost. If I had come into this meeting and said this layoff was necessary and an exciting opportunity for our company, would they trust me? Would they respect me? No, they wouldn't, because they are negatively impacted. There is not a lot that is exciting about a new process that is going to require an extra hour of paperwork every week or increasing your workload for the same pay, but that is oftentimes what you are asked to do.

In my experience, most frontline employees do not trust executive leadership. They are a nameless, faceless, interchangeable group whose only achievement is making life harder and making decisions that are hard to explain. But they can trust you, and when they do so, you will get the very best out of them. That, in and of itself, will help not only your career but theirs as well.

We have established that trust is important, but how do you earn it? You are hoping for a magic bullet, but there isn't one. Trust is earned through consistency in action. Reid Hoffman, founder of LinkedIn, likes to say it is an equation:

Trust = Consistency + Time.

It's not hard to understand: have integrity and put the team and the individuals on the team above yourself.

Your team wants to trust you. They want a good boss. Understand that trust is reciprocal; in order to gain trust, you must first give it. You will earn it through the little things. Do you need a doctor's note when someone is sick? Nope, they are an adult. Do you need to check in on progress daily after a work assignment is made? Nope, trust that they will be a professional.

Although I said that trust needs to be earned, when you come into a new team, you actually need to do the opposite—give it away. You should walk in the door trusting each individual 100 percent. Trust each individual on your team implicitly unless over time they give you a reason not to. The fastest way for them to trust you is to make sure you first demonstrate your faith in them.

LISTEN

One of the additional jobs you inherit when you become a middle manager is that of therapist. People on your team need a sounding board where they can bring their work problems and challenges. Listening to your team is one of the keys to keeping them functional. Let them whine and complain.

This can be one of the more challenging aspects of being a manager. Your team needs to be able to vent to you about the issues they are dealing with. Most of the time, you can't do anything to remove the issue, but just by the simple act of listening, you will make them feel better. One of the better bosses I had the pleasure of serving with understood the value of this. Our company had mandated some new processes I was not particularly fond of, and I was discussing those with him. "Sounds like you need to vent," he said, "so do it. You need to swear? Then go for it. That's what I am here for."

He let me know it was all right to complain to him about the issues I was seeing, so I did. It was a cathartic experience to be able to share those issues and have him just listen, even though I knew he couldn't fix anything.

Over the years, the company would mandate policy changes that were consistently unpopular. Whenever this happened, I would always receive multiple phone calls from unhappy employees. I couldn't change the policy, and they knew that; they just hoped their boss realized it was a pain to do. I did, and it was.

Hear your team. For some reason, we forget that they are people with emotions, with good days and bad days. Treat them like adults, and they will return the favor.

POINT TO BIGGER GOALS

Your team exists to solve a specific problem in the company. The key is to keep them focused on that bigger problem and not on a single bad decision. If you let them focus on this one item of stupidity, it will fester and grow into bitterness. I've watched many great employees turn into bitter low performers because they got caught focusing on the little things. Working in a large corporation means having to survive hundreds of process papercuts. They are really painful, but they will go away.

Talk about where your team contributes. Studies prove over and over again that employees who are working for a purpose are four times more likely to be engaged at work and live up to seven years longer.

As a manager, you actually have the power through your leadership to help someone live longer! That is insane. Simon Sinek has a famous TED talk about the concept of the golden circle, in which he explains the effectiveness of focusing on the "why" and not the "what." Have your team focus on why they are there, not all the little annoying things that are going on. You may not be able to adequately explain the "why" of this specific decision, but you can make sure they understand the overall "why" of the team. "Our team solves X; the rest is just noise."

True, some decisions can directly impact your ability to

solve those problems. However, this is where it is doubly important to make sure you and your team understand the primary objective of your team. It has not changed. Your goal is to keep everyone pointed to true north.

There are a couple of ways to do this. First, make sure they understand how the piece they are working on contributes to the big picture. Help them understand what their work enables. This is a challenge when you have pointless tasks to put together. For example, you have to create a Power-Point that you know no one will read for a meeting you know is pointless. This is an everyday occurrence in a lot of the teams I have been involved in. What is the value in that?

Look for the value in the peripheral. Who is going to be at the meeting? How can you sell your team? Convince your team members that the task has some redeeming value somewhere, and that will help them get through it. You should have already identified at least a few tangential values from the last chapter that will make this part easier. *Do not* pretend that the task they have to carry out is amazing; as we have already established, they are not stupid. Admit there are some challenges, but show the value in what they are being asked to do. You don't need to pretend everything is great, but you want to avoid excess negativity. Negativity breeds mediocrity.

Your team goes through the *exact* same stages that you

do when you hear a stupid decision. At first, they will push back, *à la* Chapter 1. It is your job to hear them out, then move them toward how they can make the team a success and make sure they are looking for value-adding opportunities (Chapters 2 and 3). You can guide them in the right direction because you have already planned how the message will be delivered, and you can deliver it correctly to make sure you get everyone moving forward.

Here's a quick example about a new time-tracking system that was implemented. Everyone hated it. Let's walk through how to deliver that message. First:

> *"The business wants to be able to understand what projects everyone is working on and has decided that we need to manually enter our time every week by the minute."*

This is where you will get a few grumbles and some feedback. Then:

> *"You're right; this is not going to be a fun exercise and will probably be a pain to do every week. But I can see why this will help the business better understand what everyone is doing and will give them visibility into the number of hours we are putting in and could potentially help us get more resources. I agree this is a pain, but our main goal is to get this software out on schedule, and this shouldn't affect our team's goal."*

1. Tell the "why" (even if you don't agree with the "why" or have to make one up).
2. Listen and validate (let them whine).
3. Understand how it affects them.
4. Time to move on.
5. Focus on the bigger picture.

Help your team understand that, yes, this is dumb, *but* it is small when compared to the overall team goal. Don't let the small things derail your team.

Your leadership is bigger than one bad project or bad process. We tend to focus on the here and now and think it is the most important thing in the world, but when viewed over a career, today is no more important than the day before it or the day after. How you lead your team through this single moment won't define your tenure, but it will be part of the groundwork that determines your future. It is important to take a step back, see the larger picture and (as I will talk about later) make sure they do as well. You are the leader of a team, not a project or a decision. *A team.* Lead them no matter what is going on around you.

ISOLATION STRATEGY

What about really big dumb decisions? How about a re-org? What about something you honestly can't find value in? You will be faced with this as well. This is where you need to pull the group in and make them feel like a close team. Everyone outside the group is crazy; your team members are the only sane ones. You have to find a way to keep them together. Your team bond can grow stronger through shared suffering. Psychological scientist Brock Bastian, in an article for *Psychological Science*, states, "Our findings show that pain is a particularly powerful ingredient in producing bonding and cooperation between those who share painful experiences. The findings shed light on why camaraderie may develop between soldiers or others who share difficult and painful experiences." Another article in the same journal indicated that shared pain created a "social glue" within groups.

In our case, that shared suffering could be a dumb company. Let that happen. I don't encourage the us-versus-them mentality; however, to endure the really stupid, you may be left with no choice. Your goal is a successful team. You need them together.

"Honestly," you may say, "I am not 100 percent sure why they made this decision. I am sure they had some reasons, but I am not going to worry about what they do. We are going to focus on solving the X problem and let the rest of them sort it out."

You have to ensure they are focused on what they can control; otherwise, they can spin out, get bitter, and get you in trouble. Isolate your team from the insanity that is the corporate world; otherwise, they would never get anything done! Move them past it quickly. Whatever dumb decision you are dealing with this week, don't worry—another one will show up next week. Isolate the team from the stupid. Let them focus on the job at hand, and you handle all the bureaucracy.

PEOPLE, NOT PROJECTS

Hopefully, the preceding points have led you to the primary conclusion: you are managing people, not projects. If you have nine people on your team, that means you will potentially need nine different strategies to motivate. The key to implementing a bad decision is not found in the tactics you employ; it is found in how you treat the people around you. Allowing your team to be people and have bad days can make a huge difference. If they need a sick day or need to leave a little early, let them. If they need to meet the cable guy, let them.

Giving these small concessions will make them want to run through a wall for you. This isn't my opinion; this is a scientific fact. It is the very first principle of Dr. Robert Cialdini's book *Influence: The Psychology of Persuasion*. The principle of reciprocity states that human beings are wired to want to return favors and pay back our debts. In short, to treat others as they've treated us. We can't help it.

Your team will want to return the favors you have given them, but they cannot return them in kind. They can't give you a day off or let you leave early, so they return the favor the only way they know how, which is by working harder and being loyal to you. To be clear, if you do these things expecting payback, then your team will know, and your support will not be genuine. Rather, this should just be how you deal with people. Stay in sync with your team through the implementation of this bad decision, and you will come out the other end.

KEY TAKEAWAYS

1. Focus on how this decision will affect the individuals on your team.
2. Translate the company-speak into real language.
3. The only success is through trust, which must be given to be earned.
4. Listen to your team; hear both the positive and negative feedback.
5. Keep them focused on the bigger picture and things they can control.
6. If all else fails, isolate them from the insanity.
7. Lead the people, not the projects.

ACTION TO TAKE TODAY

Set up biweekly one-on-one meetings with everyone on your team. Make sure you understand their perspectives.

CHAPTER 5

INSULATE YOURSELF FROM THE RESULTS

In the end you have to protect yourself at all times.
—Floyd Mayweather Jr.

After months of searching, I finally had found the perfect car for me. It was a beautiful sedan in the perfect shade of silver. The only problem was that it was in Minnesota and I was in Arkansas. That was a minor matter, so I clicked "Buy it now" on the online auction. I was so excited to pick up the car that I didn't want to wait for shipping, so I grabbed a one-way plane ticket and headed to Minnesota.

The car was just as I'd hoped, and I couldn't wait to get it home. I jumped in and started to drive. As I was driving home in my nice new car, right as it began to get dark, a blizzard hit. At no point during the planning of this trip had I checked the weather.

It was a complete whiteout. For those of you unacquainted with the term, it means visibility is zero, a deluge of snow with heavy winds. I couldn't even see the hood of my nice new car. At this point, I was a bit concerned. Since this was a new car, I had no supplies with me at all. No water, no blanket, no heavy jacket. I was in the middle of the interstate, with nowhere to go but forward. To make it even more interesting, I was running low on fuel.

With no visibility, I had to use the rumble strips on the side of the interstate and the GPS to guess where the road was and when a curve was coming. Driving at five miles per hour had never seemed so stressful. I knew that I couldn't just stop on the side of the road; with the dropping temperature and my lack of supplies, the odds were low I could make it through the night. As time passed, it started to dawn on me that I might be in real trouble. After what seemed like hours, I somehow made it to a hotel that wasn't full. As I stepped out of the car, the full force of minus twenty degrees and fifty-mile-per-hour wind hit me in the face. It felt like I was being repeatedly punched. I was completely unprepared for the onslaught of the cold. The short walk to the hotel door was brutal. I was so thankful to find this place of protection through the storm that I was willing to pay any price to use it. Had I not found shelter, I would have frozen to death on the side of the road.

I found myself on the lesser side of prepared, faced with a snowstorm in Minnesota, which in hindsight should have been obvious. I somehow had not considered that there might be bad weather in the middle of winter.

It should be just as obvious that over the course of your professional life, you are going to be tasked to do things that fail. Which might...freeze your career. (Did you like that analogy? You know you did.) The storm will come, and you'd better find a way to insulate yourself, or you will die on the side of the road. So let's put a few layers on to help insulate ourselves from the inevitable storm.

LAYER 1

RECENCY BIAS: TIME YOUR FAILURE

"What have you done for me lately?" It is surprisingly easier than you would think to undo something not-so-great with something great. The truth is, people around you are only going to remember your most recent results. Performance reviews are done at the end of the year. Your overall ratings are done at the end of the year as well. What do you think is more important, what you did in January or what you did in September? Your "yearly" review is based on what you do in the last few months of the year!

No, it is not fair, but it's science. Your boss doesn't magically have better control of human bias than anyone else. There is a reason people seem to work harder around review time: because it works. This is great news and bad news. The interesting takeaway is *when* you fail is just as important as how. Try not to fail in the last few months of the year. If your company is anything like mine, we have to submit our yearly performance reviews in November. So, if possible, avoid terrible projects that end in September to November.

Your overall career is subject to the exact same rules as a yearly review. Over the course of a twenty-year career, do you think anyone really remembers your success or failures in the first five? Those can affect you in the moment, but over the course of your career, it all averages out. When I was first promoted to manager, my team was given a project that I poured my heart and soul into. As a part of this project, I had to stand up in front of a room of executives and give them a readout of the project status. I prepared diligently for every question I thought they would ask. I walked in with confidence. I walked out destroyed. They asked several questions I did not have answers to, and I was sure that I came off as a fool. At that point, I felt like the world had ended and I might as well start updating my résumé.

The truth is, they forgot me when I walked out of the room. A decade later, I am 100 percent confident that the only one who remembers that presentation is me. We assume the world revolves around us and that everyone is constantly judging us. The reality is people don't really care about you that much. Take heart; you're not that memorable.

Look into the future five years from now. You are locked in a room with everyone who has worked on the project you knew would fail. What would they think? What do your peers think of you? Guess what? They don't care all that much about this project. Take a nice slow deep breath. What you are facing right now seems like a huge stumbling block, but in reality, over the course of your career, it doesn't matter as much as you think it does.

LAYER 2
BUILD THE NETWORK

You are not the only one of your colleagues that thinks this is a mistake. You need to build your network of others who know it is dumb. It is imperative that you find allies in your situation. Call up your peers one by one and get their pulse on the situation. It is *very* important you don't state your opinion until they give theirs first; they might actually be aboard the stupid train. Ask, "I can see some potential challenges with X; what do you think?" Once you gauge where they are, *then* you can go further into detail about the challenges you see.

This call is not a time for you to vent about your frustrations. You are not there to complain to them; you are merely pointing out the challenges you see. For lack of a better word, you are spreading propaganda. You are planting the seed in your peers' minds that if it does end up going south, you pointed it out.

Building a group of allies is essential for when the project eventually goes south. They will remember that you pointed out the challenges, and they could potentially help shield you from some consequences down the line. You also build allies in case you need to help persuade your boss about a course of action. Remember, you do not want to get the reputation as a complainer, which is why you need to focus on the word "challenges." Let them talk. The purpose is for you to hear their point of view and frustrations. There are several reasons why this is important:

1. You validate your own viewpoint. If you are the only one who thinks this is crazy, that may mean you're wrong.

2. You don't know who will end up where in the organization. Your peer may be your boss at some point; build those relationships now.
3. You can *share the pain.*

This is the most conclusive reason to socialize the craziness in the org. You need to make sure your peers are aware of the dumb things that are happening. You are slowly building a tribe of people who understand that you and your team are not to blame. If it does inevitably fail and the business comes down hard on you, they will all immediately empathize and be more willing to help you in the future because they believe that you have been wronged.

You are building allies in your fight against stupidity. Next time there is a crazy decision that affects them, they will come directly to you. You will have the opportunity to band together as a peer group and push back against the dumb. The more of you who have arms locked together, the better chance you will stand in the future. Build that army now. We will talk more about the importance of this and how to achieve this in Chapter 8.

LAYER 3
OVERCOMMUNICATE

The worst thing you can do is surprise your boss with the

challenges you are facing. This may mean weekly calls, weekly emails, and using every opportunity to let them know what is going on. For example, when you are crafting an update email or update status, make sure you add a section for current challenges. You don't want them to think everything is going smoothly. Use this template:

- Current Status
  - Project X is on track
- Current Challenges
  - New process has slowed our delivery time

It really is that simple, and you want to rehash challenges. Do *not* use long paragraphs. You have heard the average attention span is shortening? Well, your boss's is shorter than a two-year-old's. If any email is over a paragraph, you are doing it wrong. They won't read sentences, but they will read bullet points. They have been trained by years of PowerPoint abuse. You are not writing a novel. Stop it.

If getting things done is a challenge for the entire project, then you list them every single week. Keep it at the forefront so it is something you have identified at the beginning. You have to control the messaging, and to do that, you have to send messages! This is the CYA (cover your a$%) part, and put together with everything else we are going to talk about, it gives you the greatest chance of surviving the dumb decisions you face every day.

In the next part in your messaging, you need to make sure you accurately foreshadow the outcome. You think this process will fail? You think this project will fail? You need to get that down. Not in a heavy-handed way, *but* you need to get it in your boss's mind that you saw what was coming. This goes back to the messaging about disagreeing with your boss in Chapter 2.

Let's run through some examples.

Stupid Policy

"I think this policy may have a detrimental effect on morale. What do you think?"

Dumb Project

"Given everything we have going on, it is going to be a challenge to get this done on time. What do you think?"

Blatantly Stupid Statement

"Can you help clarify how this helps us achieve our overall goals? What do you think?"

These are soft, inoffensive statements, but they express your doubt and make it clear where you stand on the issue. Make sure to add "What do you think?" after every statement. Give your boss an opportunity to explain the "why" behind the decision. The more you let your boss talk, the better it is for you. If, three months after the decision, you are still seeing its ramifications, it is okay to point that out and list your challenges.

I was sitting on a call with my boss [director], his boss [executive director], and his boss [VP]. During the course of the meeting, the ED made a commitment to the VP that one of my projects would be completed in August, which was five weeks in the future. He made this commitment without talking to either my director or me. This was completely insane. There was a 0 percent chance of this happening. I was completely set up to fail.

To this day, I still have no idea what he was trying to do. Impress the VP? Push us harder? Didn't really matter. Either way, he had thrown down an unachievable target. My director already knew this wasn't possible. My communication: "The timeline is going to be tight, this project has 'X' challenges. It will be close, but we are working toward that goal." His response: "You have to get it done." And that was that.

I sent another email to my direct boss, letting him know that because of this new timeline, I had to shift resources, and I identified the impact on the other projects. "Given the new direction and accelerated timelines, I am shifting resources from other projects. This will give us the best opportunity to hit our target but will have the effect of significantly reducing the deliverables for project X in the next few months."

I was candid, open, and honest. I outlined the issues and impact and foreshadowed that we might not make it. More importantly, I sent detailed weekly status updates to let them know where we were.

They were not happy when we did not make the deadline, but they were not surprised.

LAYER 4
BUILD A LEARNING NARRATIVE

If you learn anything from this entire book, let it be this: build a learning narrative. This is the absolute most important thing you can do to insulate yourself from getting a bad label that follows you around.

Why? Just as we talked about in the previous chapters, people want *solutions*, not problems. This is where you bring them those solutions. Remember when we talked about how everyone has a boss? Well, when your team fails, your boss is more upset because now they have to go tell their boss why something failed. You have to give them something positive to take with them to those meetings. You are going to fail a lot over your career due to bad decisions. So let's dig in.

What is a learning narrative? After the failure, you need to communicate explicitly what you believe led to the failure. But most important, communicate steps you think can be taken to prevent the same failure next time.

Remember the project I just talked about in the previous section? Big surprise, I didn't make it. I had already foreshadowed that outcome and listed the challenges, which was in my favor. The communication was that I was going to "fail" at meeting this new, unrealistic deadline.

> "Project X is not going to meet the August first deadline and will be pushed three weeks to August twenty-first. This is due in no small part to the amount of work we uncovered once we got into the database. We can mitigate this issue in the future by doing deeper analysis and scoping at the beginning of the project to determine work effort and number of resources needed."

Notice I didn't say, "Because you set an unrealistic deadline." That's the real reason, but they don't care, so no point pushing that button. The key is that you identify actionable steps that can be taken to mitigate this risk going forward. Is this going to make everything somehow better immediately? *Nope.* It will, however, soften the blow and help you don the mantle of someone who is solving problems. Someone else made the decision that led to your failure, but that is irrelevant. You will be the one who is blamed if it does fail, so you have to be prepared to handle the aftermath.

LAYER 5
THE REBOUND

When you have been in a long-term relationship with someone, it really sucks to get dumped. So, what do we as humans do? We jump back into a relationship as fast as we can to dull the pain and pick up the easy win. Someone likes us again! There is hope in the world!

When your company dumps on you and you fail, you need to go get a quick win. Remember recency bias? You need to do something to get the failure stink off of you quickly. Grab a rebound task. It is a short-term win that can slowly chip away at the thing that failed. It is not something big and grand; it is something small.

For instance, every week, my boss will ask for some sort of information. "Can you get me this PowerPoint by Friday?" Get it to him by Wednesday. *Win.* "Can you provide that document by the end of the day?" Do it immediately. *Win.* All the tasks that are beneath you and stupid? Do them with renewed vigor. Then you become the person they can count on. The recency bias begins to kick in in a big way. You don't know when the next layoff is coming, so be ready. If you are already doing those things, then *great!*

Just like the rest of corporate drones, you have too much work on your plate, right? This one decision, be it a project or a new process, should not be the only thing you are executing on. You need to find ancillary work. Maybe it is volunteering to run a call or even volunteering to take on another problem. Ensure that you have more on your to-do list than this one bad decision. That way, when this decision goes sour, it is sandwiched in between other good work.

I know the thought of taking on more work when you are overwhelmed seems like a terrible idea, but this is about survival, not making yourself comfortable. As we talked about in the previous chapters, you do this by looking for others' pain points. Look for other ways to solve their problems. If you solve problems for others, you will be employed for a very long time.

Another important key is to make sure you are highlighting your accomplishments and wins in the weekly updates and staff meetings. Make sure to say "my team" has accomplished this and "my team" has completed this. When you are giving credit to others, it no longer sounds like incessant bragging because you are inclusive of that team. Those rebound wins are starting to help the recency bias. Go out and start getting some rebound wins as fast as you can. More bad decisions are coming, so start to tip the scale in your favor.

You must be prepared to recover quickly when the failures show up.

Recency bias is just that, a bias, but it is one that can be used in your favor if you understand how it works.

- Make sure you are socializing with your peers and being the one they turn to when they need to talk about work issues.
- Never surprise your leaders; make sure you are over-communicating what is happening in your projects.
- Never leave them empty-handed, trying to explain why your team couldn't get it done. If you do, they will just make something up.
- Have a solid lesson learned and concrete steps that can be taken to mitigate those risks in the future.
- Finally, always be looking for new tasks you can take on that can get a few things in the win column.

No matter what happens, there will always be some blowback when a goal is not achieved. If you follow these rules, you can effectively insulate yourself from the worst of the damage. The key, when the storm comes, is just to continue to drive forward, even if it is only at five miles an hour. Don't stop.

KEY TAKEAWAYS

1. Focus on being prepared and protecting yourself for the inevitable storm.
2. When you fail can be just as important as why you fail.
3. Build a network of allies that can be used today or useful in the future.
4. Never let your boss be surprised by anything; over-communicate everything.
5. Spin a positive impression by building a learning narrative out of failure.
6. Find a quick win after a failure to allow human bias to kick in.

ACTION TO TAKE TODAY

Assess yourself. Are you making sure to follow these rules? Overcommunicating? Building a learning narrative? Are you ready for a storm?

CHAPTER 6

REALITY IS IRRELEVANT

*Perception is reality. If you are perceived to
be something, you might as well be it because
that's the truth in people's minds.*

—STEVE YOUNG

I was a model employee. I put in extra hours and vol-
unteered for the extra assignments nobody wanted. I
took great pride in my work, making sure everything was
completed ahead of schedule and at the highest quality.
I was following all the advice I had been given on how to
move up the corporate ladder and be successful.

When it came time for my yearly review, I sat down
with my manager and was genuinely excited to hear his
feedback. He went through my accomplishments for the
year and noted that my performance had been fantastic.

At the conclusion of the review, I asked him if there was anything I could be doing better. He thought for a moment and said he couldn't think of anything. I pressed him; surely there was something I could improve.

"Well, twice a week you are taking long lunches, and that is giving the perception to your peers you are not putting in enough effort."

I was floored. It was true; on Tuesdays and Thursdays I took an hour-and-a-half lunch to play racquetball with another employee. What's more, my manager is actually the one who gave me permission to do this! My results didn't matter. My work ethic didn't matter. *All* that mattered was other people's *perception*. This was a hard lesson to learn. Concerned about the repercussions of this perception, I never played racquetball at lunch again.

To succeed in the corporate world, the only thing that actually matters is other people's perception. In order to be successful, you have to learn how to influence the perception of those around you. You do this by understanding a few basics on how those opinions are formed in the mind. What emotional impact do you want to convey? How do you want people to remember you? Take control of how people perceive you so that they form a positive mental image of you that will last for years. Let's talk about how to make that happen.

MAKE THEM FEEL IMPORTANT

There are a few emotions that override our thought processes. One is the feeling of value. People *love* to feel important. Admit it. You feel the same way. The easiest way to show someone they are important is to value their time over yours.

What does his mean, practically? Show up for meetings on time. Nothing is worse than showing up late for a meeting. When you show up late, you are conveying the message that your time is more valuable than everyone else's on the call. *Don't do it.*

I can't tell you how many comments I have personally gotten about my promptness. It makes a huge difference when you automatically put others' time first. When you are scheduling meetings with someone, make every effort to schedule a time that works for them. That includes people who are above and below you on the org chart. You are building a narrative. You are building an emotional connection that you value their time. In the world of back-to-back and overlapping meetings, this is really difficult to do. Pick the meetings you are going to beforehand; for the ones you can't, notify the organizers that you will not be able to attend. Always let people know the moment you know you will be a few minutes late. This is an easy step to start anchoring those emotional responses.

Tell them you appreciate and respect their opinions. In previous chapters, we have talked about how important it is for you to ask your boss's opinion. The same holds true of others in your organization.

You might think this is just sucking up. It's not. Why? Because you *should* be valuing their opinion. There is that word again, "value." Make them feel important. Ask them for their opinion. *Listen* and then *respond* that you heard them and repeat their opinion back to them. "I appreciate your perspective on this; those are some valid points..." Then you can go into your point, whether you agree or not. Let them be heard first. This is setting the stage for when they see you a year from now. You've dropped that subconscious emotional anchor, so they think, *I liked working with him.* They may not even know why, but it is because you made them feel important, put their time above your own, and listened to what they had to say.

TO BE PRAISED

People like to feel important. You know what else people love? *Credit.* Especially in a business setting. Everyone in an organization wants to make sure their work gets credit, that their contributions are recognized, and that they add value.

One of the biggest annoyances in corporate culture is

PowerPoint plagiarism. You make a PP for your boss with all your info and your work. He presents it...then gets all the credit. I imagine you can think of several examples where others took credit for someone else's work.

I remember a director walking up to one of his managers and asking, "Hey, I need to do a presentation on our latest results; can you send me the slides you had?" The manager replied, "Sure, but keep my name on them so I can get credit."

I was shocked at the gall of this manager, but his boss said okay, and his name stayed. He had finally gotten tired of his boss taking credit for making the slides.

Everyone wants the credit. So give it to them. Make sure every success is because of your team. Make sure you laud your peers for anything they do well. You see someone in person with a tangential project, tell them "good job." Seems small, but this is *huge* in creating the emotional anchor that will serve you in the long term when everything blows up in your face. So much of what you do from day to day is going to be a thankless job. Make sure you are the anomaly who says "Thanks."

SNAP PERCEPTION

I will highlight it again for emphasis:

> Your results don't matter. It is people's perception of you and your work that determines the course of your career.

I was going through the gamut of interviewing several internal candidates for an open position. I had two solid candidates, and I knew both of their previous managers, so I gave them a quick call to see how they felt about the individuals. For one candidate, I was told they were a solid employee. For the other one, I was told that he was "high maintenance." I poked a little further, just to make sure it wasn't a personality clash. This candidate had a habit of causing more problems than he solved. That is not something I wanted to take a chance on. Remember, you are *not* judged on your résumé. You are judged on the perception of people who work with you.

People tend to get touchy about this subject because we all like to think we are some beacon of impartiality. You are not. Is it fair? No. But we are humans; this is how it works. You are judged every time you walk into a room. You are judged every time you open your mouth. It is not intentional; it is human nature. Embrace the insanity, understand this, and use it to your advantage.

As humans, we have evolved to make snap judgments. First impressions are not something we can really control, as they are actually done by our unconscious brain.

In one study published in *Social Psychological and Personality Science*, individuals were shown photographs of a person and told to make judgments about the person. Questions included: Are they open? Are they agreeable? Do you like them? They rated all these characteristics based on a photograph! Then participants met those same people in person and interacted with them for thirty minutes, talking and playing a game. Then they rerated them. The score from the pictures and the real-life interactions were basically a match! The only thing that changed was whether the participants thought the people from the pictures were extroverts or not.

This is nuts, but it does tell you one thing you already knew: you are judged on your looks and body language. Immediately. Your team immediately has decided what they think of you as soon as you walk into a room! There's a thought that is not so comforting in our PC world. People care how you look and how you present yourself. You cannot control these snap judgments, but you can be aware of their impact and plan for them.

DO THEY LIKE YOU?

When I was in first grade, there was a guy I couldn't stand. He was bigger than everyone and liked to pick on other kids. We got into several fights. I saw him when I was an adult. Before we even spoke a word to one another, I knew I still didn't like the guy. Why? Could I remember anything we argued or fought about when we were six years old? Did I have *any* recent facts to back up how I felt?

Nope. It was simply because I remembered the emotions I had when I saw that person. How we perceived the world when we were children still influences us even when we become adults. That is how long these emotional responses can stay with us. The facts fade away. *All* we remember are emotions. We create emotional anchors to our memories of people. Emotions play a huge role in creating our memories, how we store those memories, and how easily we can recall them. You do it. I do it. We all do it. That is why we can recall so easily where we were when a traumatic event happened, such as September 11.

A huge part of your career is what people feel about you because that is what they will remember. They will forget what you produce. They will forget the long hours you work, but they *will* remember how they feel about you! They will remember if they liked working with you. Seems ridiculous, right? Everyone wants to be judged fairly based on their results. Put that out of your mind right now. *It is scientifically impossible* for humans to make emotion-free judgments. How do you want them to remember you?

Your focus needs to be on generating good emotional connections in others. "Spontaneous trait transference" is the concept we want to employ; people will associate adjectives you use to describe other people with your own personality. According to Gretchen Rubin, author of the book *The Happiness Project*,

> "whatever you say about other people influences how people see you. If you describe a co-worker as brilliant and charismatic, your acquaintance will tend to associate you with those qualities. Conversely, if you describe a co-worker as arrogant and obnoxious, those traits will stick to you. So, watch what you say."

One study published in the *Journal of Personality and Social Psychology* found that this effect occurred even when people knew certain traits didn't describe the people who had talked about them. Simply put, if you are spreading negativity, you are only damaging yourself. Yes, I am telling you that in order to be successful, you need to be nicer.

AVOIDING NEGATIVE PERCEPTIONS

Stop pretending to be busy. Just stop it. Stop right now. No one cares that you are busy. We are all busy.

This is how a normal conversation starts with so many coworkers that I know, "Hey, how's it going?"

"Man, I am so slammed right now."

Why do we feel the need to let people know that we are busy? This contributes to a negative perception of being overwhelmed. You do not want to get that label. Do you think your boss or your peers care if you are "busy"? We have already been through this. What do they care about? Are you solving a problem they have? That's it. Are you really busy? Most of us know people that are "slammed" yet have time at work to check Facebook for an hour or hang out in the break room. We have lost all reference in the white-collar world of what it means to be busy.

So how should you handle those interactions? Use specifics instead of generalities. "I have this new project that seems to really be taking off," or "There are a lot of meetings about X." Don't be generic. If your boss asks you about your workload (which rarely ever happens), the answer is, "Here are the things I currently have on my to-do list right now. It's a lot, but I am working through it."

In large companies, the odds of getting more resources are slim. The goal with these interactions is to influence the perception of control. Do you think your boss will give you more responsibility if you are "so busy"? Others should come away from an interaction with you with the feeling that you have everything taken care of.

If you are assigned more tasks than you can handle, be honest about the trade-offs: "Since this has been added to my list, it is going to take some of my time off of X." They may not always like to hear it, but that is part of the candid feedback.

I led one large software development project with fifteen-plus developers. After six months, another project with an even bigger size and scope was dropped in my lap, with an aggressive deadline. I was very up front with the trade-off this would pose. I was already working fifty hours a week; this new project also needed fifty. It was easy to see that math was not going to work out in my favor. I was candid with my leadership about the challenges this posed and asked how I could best prioritize my time. I pushed a little further and asked, "If both break at the same time, which one do I fix?" I got my answer and knew where to shift my time. Conflicting priorities require trade-offs, and that is okay as long as they are communicated adequately.

BE HEARD

Do you like to hang out in the back row and just keep your head down and get your job done? That's great; enjoy getting laid off.

Your job is to win the stack-rank game. When it comes

time for your boss to lay someone off, what happens? They stack rank you with all your peers. When it is time to hand out raises, stack rank. Opportunities for promotion, stack rank. This all plays into the perception angle. What do they perceive in you?

Make no mistake, you are marketing yourself and building a personal brand. You are doing that by building an emotional attachment to the memories people have of you. In a large meeting, never be the first one to ask a question, but always ask a question. The most irritating thing I ever saw in my career was an engineer who would always ask these really deep questions that didn't mean anything, but it gave him the appearance of being very intelligent. "This is interesting; I would like to see how this would interact with our current models." He raised his hand to say that. Wasn't even a question. Worse, if you asked him a question, he would talk for a while and never give an answer; "Glad you brought that up, we definitely need to consider that from all angles and determine the best way forward."

He got promoted. Guy accomplished nothing but was a genius at playing the game. It was only with the benefit of hindsight that I could appreciate the strategy he employed.

You have to be present. You have to be heard. Ask

questions and make yourself present. If you have an opportunity to sit in a town hall and ask a question, never ask something about yourself or your team. Ask a question about the business. "We are seeing a lot of mergers; what is your observation on how it may potentially affect our strategy?" You want to ask the questions that they get on Bloomberg and CNN all the time. You show them you are concerned about the bigger picture.

Once again, always ask for their opinion. Same with other meetings. Ask for others' opinions. People love the sound of their own voice. This isn't just to placate them; by really listening, you will gain valuable insight, and you will stop yourself from saying something potentially stupid about something you don't know about.

You read the story at the beginning of this chapter where I learned about the value of perception. Let's fast-forward ten years. I walked into my boss's office ready to receive my yearly review. I was feeling pretty confident, having blown past every single goal we had laid out at the beginning of the year. I expected a "Leading," which is the highest rating one can get and leads to a bigger raise.

My expectations were quickly deflated, as I was just "Performing." I sat in stunned silence as my boss rattled off my accomplishments. I waited for him to finish. After listening to my list of stellar results, I paused for a moment, then asked, "Where did I fall short? What can I do to improve?" Well, he couldn't actually think of anything!

Is this starting to sound familiar? I pressed a little more. He said, "Well, I wanted to give you a Leading rating, but another director was not in agreement." Yes, you heard that right! I needed to convince other directors, whom I didn't work with and didn't speak to, in order to get a good review. *Perception.* It got me again ten years later!

You *must* do the things in this chapter to build the emotional attachment, so when a bunch of leaders sit in a room and talk about you, there is a positive feeling. They will have *no* idea what your actual accomplishments are, *yet* they hold your career in their hands. Make the emotional attachment. Control the perception.

KEY TAKEAWAYS

1. Your results don't matter. It is people's perception of you and your results that determines your career.

2. Make everyone feel important by valuing their time and their opinion.

3. People love to be praised, so don't hold back.

4. Every human being in the world makes snap judgments. Be prepared for this and be ready to influence them.

5. Avoid negative perception by telegraphing that you have everything under control.

6. Don't hide. In order to create emotional attachment, you have to speak up.

ACTION TO TAKE TODAY

Identify the emotional impact you want to convey. Make a baseline of where you think you are today and write down what behaviors you can change to make the biggest impact on others' perception of you.

CHAPTER 7

WHAT IF YOU ARE WRONG?

Whenever I'm about to do something, I think, "Would an idiot do that?" And if they would, I do not do that thing.

—Dwight Schrute

I came into a role as the leader of an established team. Like most leaders, in my arrogance, I thought I could make it better. I needed to make my mark, so naturally I instituted some new processes on how we prioritize work in our queue. I admit it; I felt good about it.

I did this without taking the time to actually validate whether my plan was good or not. In doing so, I made myself the bottleneck. As I was a new boss, team members were reluctant to speak out against my bad idea.

It only took a few weeks to see that what I had created

was awful. I could have easily brushed it off or even doubled down. Thankfully, I had a blast of sanity and realized I had made everything worse. I called together a team meeting. I started the meeting with a mea culpa.

"This new process that I started isn't working."

What ideas did the team have to make it better? After a brief moment of silence, voices started to chime in. Working together, we came up with a much more efficient process. Why I didn't ask for this feedback from the start, I have no idea. I was being an idiot.

We have already talked about how hard it is to change someone's mind. In addition, most of us tend to hold on to our ideas to the last possible moment, even when presented with alternative facts. This chapter is about the hardest skill to master: self-awareness. You have to be smart enough to know when you have a failing position, cash in your chips, and get out. Those who dogmatically hold on to an idea are not long for their jobs.

A common misconception is that Darwin put forth the theory that the strong survive. In reality, what he found is that those who adapt survive. You have to be willing to adapt to the situation around you, especially when the information changes. How you handle what comes next after you are wrong determines how large an impact it will be. The good news? It doesn't matter as much as you think; right or wrong, you can win either way!

PEOPLE LIKE MISTAKES

When you make a mistake, the most common reaction is to ignore it and hope it just goes away. You are afraid of how this will make you look. This is a natural reaction. However, studies show that this would be a mistake in itself.

Embrace the fact that you were wrong. Everyone already knows you screwed up, and attempting to hide that fact is not going to make any difference. For Father's Day, my wife had our kids write down all the things they loved about me. Among all the wonderful statements about how amazing and strong I am, my eight-year-old daughter wrote, "Daddy admits when he makes a mistake." This was powerful to me because even my daughter could see that I was trying to live with humility.

Admitting when you make a mistake is powerful. It is not a weakness. It conjures an emotional reaction in people's memory. It can be part of the process of creating that emotional anchor. Study after study proves that humility is one of the top traits of an effective leader. Making a mistake and then being open and honest about it will actually make your team work harder! Your team will actually like you better if you fail! That's a pretty big win.

Most leaders are afraid to admit and embrace their mistakes. Not Warren Buffett. You will notice something interesting in his annual letter to stakeholders. One of the first things he does is talk about something that he did wrong. He doesn't hide it or bury it; he brings it out right up front. Sometimes he is so successful he doesn't even have anything to write for that year, so he talks about mistakes he made in the past instead! He understands the principles of humility and establishes his credibility immediately.

I started a brand-new project using the worst method possible; I immediately jumped to a conclusion. I looked at the problem, quickly sized it up, and came up with a solution. I was very confident in how smart I was and that I had finally solved this issue that had been plaguing the company for years! I was really shocked that no one had thought of this before. It was obvious to me at this point that no one had solved it because, well, I am a genius. I talked up my solution to several people without doing the legwork to validate that I was, in fact, right. I even made the cardinal sin of putting it on a PowerPoint! That's right, a PowerPoint—there was no going back now.

My executive sponsor for the project said I needed to get more evidence and keep digging. This seemed a bit silly to me since I had already figured it out. I spent the next two months going through the Lean Six Sigma process to prove my original hypothesis. I was fully absorbed in confirmation bias at this point, and somehow only managed to find the facts that fit the narrative that I wanted to tell. Turns out if you work hard enough, you can make the data say anything you want to.

Given the title of this chapter, I think I may have foreshadowed the outcome. I stood in front of those same executives and presented my bulletproof logic. Sadly, my logic may have been bulletproof, but it was not bombproof. It didn't take long for the well-seasoned execs to spot the flaws in my reasoning. Not only was I wrong, but what I thought was the root cause wasn't even remotely connected! I had been proven wrong in a very public way. I was the idiot.

Researcher Elliot Aronson discovered the phenomenon of the pratfall effect. He studied how simple mistakes affect our perceived likability. He asked male students to listen to individuals taking a quiz. When the individuals did well on the quiz but spilled coffee at the end of the interview, the students rated them higher in likability. His research discovered that committing a mistake would actually make a person more likable. The mistake humanizes a person and makes us want to be around them!

Mistakes are not as terrible as we make them out to be.

Think about the people in your office who have been promoted. Are they perfect? I would imagine you don't have to work very hard to spot the flaws in everyone that is promoted instead of you. Yet we walk around afraid to be exposed. Stop it. You will be wrong and make mistakes in your career. Own them and move on.

In the stock market, there is a term known as a "stop-loss." If a stock you are invested in starts to drop, you can set a floor price you want to sell at so you don't lose everything. Many times, this can be used to take the emotional component out of investing. You decide at what point you need to get out before everything gets worse.

The principle is the same with your career. Set your stop-loss number. You have prepared for this to fail, but when you see positive signs (hey, it's actually working!), get out of your losing position. For example, your company put out an expense policy you are against, yet you start to see all the savings happening. Just as we talked about in Chapter 2, see it from the other angle. When you start to see some of those claimed benefits, talk them up! Praise them to leadership and peers. Don't keep silent. You can play the stop-loss game. If you start to see the value of the decision going up, then it's time to sell your incorrect position!

CREDIT WHERE IT IS DUE

The same concepts from the perception chapter are applicable in this situation. We already talked about how people like to be praised. Do you know what people love more than anything? They want to feel like a genius. Give them that. Through the investigation you have done on the initial decision, you know where everyone stands. You want to make a point of letting them know personally that they were correct. They know it and they *love* to hear it. It is not blatant or brownnosing. They were right; you were wrong. You owe them that.

You don't even have to admit you were wrong in every conversation; it is implicit: "Great call on the new process; it has really changed things." "You were right, this new strategy seems to really be paying off."

This also ties into what we talked about in the last chapter with emotional connection. They will not remember this in two years, but they will remember how you made them feel. When someone is told they are right, they feel great, and that feeling is now tied to you!

Dave Thomas, the founder of Wendy's, said it best: "The one thing people remember about you isn't how much money you make or the deals you swung. What they remember is if you were a nice guy."

Don't hold back praise when others are right. Don't make a point of avoiding it; talk about it with your peers and be gracious in defeat. Compliment those who made the right call—even if it is your boss. On a side call, tell them you were impressed with leadership's execution of this decision and it turned out to be a great idea. Now this seems counterintuitive, but I promise—it works every single time.

Good example: "Wow, I am really impressed with how well they executed this. Everyone did a great job."

That's it! Simple and to the point. Do not make excuses and do not point out specifically what you missed. You were opposed and now you see it as valuable; that is the only narrative that you need to convey. Remember, you are fighting a war of perception; make your boss remember that you came around.

Bad example: "I can't believe that worked, *but* they got a lot of help from executives."

Don't make excuses about why it was successful. We try to do this to save face, but in reality, it just comes off as sour grapes. You can do your own personal introspection to see what you may have missed or what variables changed. In public, it is unnecessary and can be counterproductive.

DON'T FIGHT

The truth is there will be those in your career that want to see you fail. Some people rejoice in others' failures. In their mind, their success depends on your downfall. Remember, they are fighting the stack-rank game as well. If you get called out by a peer or even a boss, do not fight it.

I realize this is a tough statement to hear. As someone who is driven to be successful and cares about your reputation, you have to shut off your fight instinct. Do not claim you had false information or try to justify your skepticism in any way. Resist the urge to debate; you will be giving them ammo they need to fuel their impression of you. You must counter with admission. "Yep, you're right; I was skeptical, but I have been impressed—this has been great." This should be delivered with enthusiasm, not with a defeatist attitude. In doing so, you will completely disarm them.

Have you ever tried to have an argument with someone who has a positive attitude? I promise, it is the most irritating thing in the world. If you have a positive attitude, there is no next step they can take to push the conversation further. They will also, more than likely, try to tear you down in a group setting, which is why it is even more important to react appropriately.

In the last chapter, we talked a lot about controlling the

narrative. You have that ability when you are wrong as well. It is so important to remember that you are playing the long game. Just like we talked about in the early chapters, they won't remember this conversation; they will remember the emotions surrounding it. They won't remember your words, but they will remember how you delivered them.

You can't do anything about negative people at your job. If you are at all successful, you will create rivals through their jealousy. Can't be stopped, but because they are people, they can be managed. The key to winning is humility and the right attitude.

DON'T BE AFRAID TO LOOK STUPID

Most project management teams use a stoplight chart to let the executives know the status of ongoing projects. Green means good, yellow means caution, and red means behind schedule. We were working on a highly visible project that was not going well. Our project manager was fairly new to the role and seemed a bit overwhelmed by it all. We communicated to him that we might not make our deadline, so we should be in a "yellow" status. He listened intently, and then went and reported everything as "green."

The next week we told him the same thing—and he proceeded to present a PowerPoint to our executives with a "green" status. We were not happy with this development, as we felt it was going to backfire.

We got to the last few weeks of the project, and it was clear we were not going to make our deadline. Then he decided to communicate to the execs that our team had hit a snag and that everything would have to be pushed for a few weeks. They were angry at us for not hitting the target. They immediately called and started demanding to know why they were not aware of this delay sooner, as it had to be coordinated with our marketing teams. We politely informed them that we had communicated our status, but the PM decided to change it.

The PM was now the one who was on the receiving end of a sharp reprimand. At this point, we hoped he had gotten the message about what a terrible idea this was to not report the truth. Instead, he moved the deadline out two weeks and reported us as "green" for the new deadline. He was so terrified to go in and report that the project was having delays that he avoided it. He tried hard to cover up the failures of the project, hoping they could be dealt with at some time in the future.

One of the challenges I have seen in many careers is people who are afraid to be wrong. They are afraid to be called out. So they stand for nothing and accomplish nothing. This is not going to help you when stack-rank comes around. What you need to get from this chapter specifically is that even if you are wrong, you can still win. You can still turn it in your favor.

Don't worry about looking stupid. What you should worry about is the person who is completely forgettable who has no defining traits. The one they don't think about is the one who gets laid off. The one who is ignored for promotions. Stand for something and don't worry if you are wrong. Navigate that when it comes to pass, using the tips we have talked about, and you can ensure that if this time you were the idiot, no one will remember. The fear of failure is not what holds people back. It is the fear of other people finding out about your failure that stops you. It will hold back careers and great accomplishments. Don't let it define you, because in the long run, no one really cares.

YOU DON'T KNOW EVERYTHING

There is one other important concept for you to grasp: your boss doesn't tell you everything. There may be pieces of information that truly explain the bad decision clearly. Maybe you are getting ready for an IPO, or a huge reorganization is coming. There are hundreds of pieces of the puzzle that you are missing that went into the decision matrix. You will not be able to fully discern the origin of some of the terrible decisions you come across. Had you been given those missing strands of information, you might actually realize that you are the one who is wrong! (I mean, probably not, but it happens.)

So many times, executives are operating at a higher level than we realize. They have access to information that, when viewed in the right light, can change the perspective on decisions. You walk in and talk to them about a great new policy idea, and you're shocked when they do nothing with it. "That guy is an idiot," you mutter under your breath as you walk out, not realizing he isn't allowed to do anything about it because in three months, he won't be your boss. He already knows a re-org is coming, and he can't make that decision.

We pass judgment with insufficient facts. We are constantly walking around with asymmetric information yet assuming we know everything. We think everyone around us is an idiot when, in fact, they just have more information than we do. This attitude causes us to be arrogant and assume we have it all figured out.

> "My dog thinks I am dumb because she is clearly telling me to go outside and I am not doing it. The dog doesn't know I have other priorities."
> —SCOTT ADAMS (CREATOR OF *DILBERT*)

I was so sure of my conclusion on that Lean Six Sigma project that I put it on a PowerPoint as the root cause. Then I presented it to a bunch of VPs with no supporting facts, just my opinion. I was faced with a very real dilemma when I was wrong. I had to walk in and do another final presentation. Do I ignore my old conclusion? Try to breeze by it?

I decided to actually list it again. I said, "Here was the quick, easy conclusion, but through the process and investigating the results, this is what we actually found." I embraced the false hypothesis and created the narrative that I wanted them to see. I had learned from my mistake. I had not dogmatically stood by a bad decision.

Mistakes will happen, and sometimes you will be the one to make them. Whether it was bad information or just bad judgment, it doesn't really matter. If you embrace that mistake and don't hide from it, you can push your career forward. Focus on being humble and failing with a positive attitude. Acknowledge the mistake and then move on to something else. Use this as another opportunity to create a positive impression of yourself.

KEY TAKEAWAYS

1. Don't ignore your mistake. Own it.

2. Give credit to those who saw the situation correctly.

3. Don't fight others who would tear you down. Let them bring themselves down.

4. Don't let fear of other people's judgment hold you back.

5. You may be missing key pieces of information, which can lead to incorrect conclusions.

ACTION TO TAKE TODAY

Don't be an idiot, but if you happen to be an idiot, don't hide from it.

CHAPTER 8

THIS WILL HAPPEN AGAIN

My decision-making skills closely resemble
that of a squirrel trying to cross the street.

—UNKNOWN

Here's a story from Jan Harold Brunvand's book *The Encyclopedia of Urban Legends*: A woman was driving to her son's show-and-tell lesson with a pet gerbil in a box by her side. It escapes and begins to crawl up her pant leg. She pulls over, gets out of the car, and proceeds to jump up and down and shake her leg in order to get rid of the animal. A passerby thinks she is having a seizure, so he approaches and wraps his arms around her to calm her down. Another passerby sees the struggle, and assuming the first passerby is an attacker, punches him in the face. The woman then attempts to explain what really happened.

We all jump to conclusions without making sure we have all the correct facts. The pace of the business world today gives us the impression that we need to hurry! Our competition is coming! There is no time for further analysis; make a decision now! We spring into action, sometimes to our own detriment. In this scenario, you are the good Samaritan. You see a problem, and you will rush to help with great ideas! Then an executive will come along and punch you in the face.

Everything in this book should lead you to one simple yet dramatic conclusion: this will happen again! Humans are terrible at making business decisions. We are full of cognitive bias that ensured our survival as a species but doesn't translate quite as well to the boardroom.

You have but one choice: prepare yourself for the inevitable. Recognize that these bad decisions are not isolated incidents; they are a natural by-product of humans under stress. You will have to protect your career and yourself from this. If left unprotected, you will be sidelined or, worse, let go. Let's review where some of these bad decisions originate and what we can do to prepare before things go bad.

WHERE BAD DECISIONS COME FROM
EXPERIENCE

Decision-making is a fascinating science. Our brains have evolved to be able to make decisions quickly. Our brains are also lazy and don't want to work that hard. We take shortcuts, looking for key indicators so that we can survive. When we were living in caves in fight-or-flight mode, do you think we had time for a committee meeting or a conference call? I can't help but picture a bunch of Neanderthals huddled around a PowerPoint presentation on how to avoid a lion. We decide things based on our past experience with biases intact. This allows us to make decisions quickly without using up too many mental resources. A lion is bad. If you see a lion, run; no other input needed.

We use that cumulative experience to make faster decisions. The problem is, what if our past experience is wrong? Or not applicable? Most leaders have been promoted due to their past success. The higher up they go, the more they believe in themselves. Promotions are a confirmation that they are doing things the right way. It takes a special leader to be able to ignore experience bias and choose another path. Most of the leaders in your company are not capable of this. Not to knock them; it is just a mathematical probability that they are applying old logic to a new problem. Not their fault; it's science. As long as our brains work this way, bad decisions will keep coming.

EFFECTIVE DECISION DISTANCE

The farther away you are from the impacts of that decision, the worse it will be. The largest challenge is that executives don't have to live the impacts of their own decisions.

Executives often lack the understanding of how their decision will be received and how it will be executed. The truth is everyone in the organization only has visibility to one level above and below them. This causes blind spots and gaps in information that contribute to poor decisions. The only remedy for this is to get input from the individuals who will actually need to implement the decision. It's a step that is largely forgotten or ignored.

Let me give you an example. A company is trying to save money. A decision is made to lower the amount of money people can use for food while traveling. Instead of allowing fifty dollars per day and trusting us to make good decisions, they decide it is now a per-meal allowance. For breakfast we get eight dollars, lunch fifteen dollars, and dinner twenty-five dollars. Seems somewhat reasonable. Except that also includes tax and tip. Ever tried to eat at an airport? The prices are a bit inflated. When you start looking at it, you realize you will be eating fast food. Now, do you think the VPs and above abide by this same policy they enacted? Nope. What is the by-product of this policy? Everyone who is traveling is now stressed

EFFECTIVE DECISION DISTANCE

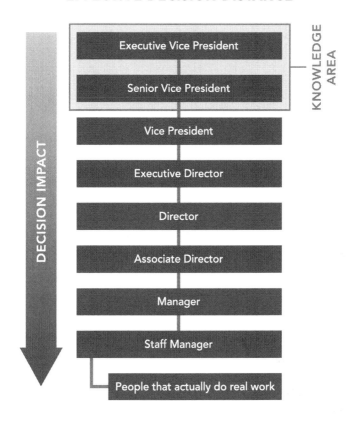

about where to eat and counting every penny, not to mention the extra time it takes to maintain all the paperwork. *They trust me to manage a team of nineteen people and make decisions that impact millions of dollars of spending, but they are worried I am not responsible enough with... breakfast.* From their spreadsheet, it makes sense that we can lower our food cost, but they are unaware of the unintended consequences of their decision.

The farther you are from the effects of the problems, the worse decisions you are going to make.

SAFETY

Its fourth and one and the team is clinging to a narrow margin of victory. What should the coach do? Should he go for it and, if he makes it, guarantee a victory, or should he punt and hope his defense can save the day? He grabs his visor and wipes the sweat from his face. He can hear the roar of the fans directly behind him. If the team wins, then he will be hailed a hero, but the fans will turn on him at a moment's notice if he messes this up. So he punts because he is scared.

In American football, coaches almost always punt on fourth down, even though statistically it is a bad decision. Why? Because they are scared. They are scared what will happen if they don't get it. The fan base will turn on them, and they will be endlessly mocked and ridiculed. If they somehow achieve a first down, the fans will love them and call them gutsy. The data tells us that the odds of converting are at least 63 percent. This is not a high-risk play. In fact, it is far riskier to give the other team the ball. Do we let the data drive our decisions? Nope, we punt. Self-preservation and fear of failure kicks in, and just as in everything else, we take the safe choice.

Everyone takes the easiest path. When it comes right down to it, the only thing people really care about is... wait for it...themselves. Mind-blowing, right? People have a ridiculous self-preservation instinct, especially those who have had a long career and are making in excess of six figures. Those are a lot of zeros that no one wants to let get away! So they will make the easy decisions and take the shortest path to guaranteed positive reviews.

Companies make these types of decisions every day. "We need to control costs, so let's cut our travel and food spending." It is an easy win. The hard path would be to actually talk to the people impacted and understand all the ripple effects that this type of policy change would have, including the long-term implications. They don't do this because very few get fired for making the safe choice. People know that.

Can we really blame them? I certainly understand the self-preservation instinct. Two people come into your office to interview for a job (Bill and Ted). Exact same credentials, both of them have solid résumés. Bill has a good interview; Ted has a great one. But Bill has a recommendation from one of your peers. You will hire Bill. He is the safe choice, the one who gives you a better guarantee of a positive outcome *even* if you think Ted might be a better hire. Nine out of ten times, Bill is getting the job. We will always take the shortest path to perceived success.

Sitting in the meeting with company leadership, they ask, "What should we do?"

"Let's cut the training budget." Safe choice. Your bosses are always going to punt.

FEAR

It was a beautiful summer day. As I walked inside the house, I realized the air conditioner was no longer working. This is not a fun thing to learn when it is over ninety degrees outside. Having no ability to fix it myself, I immediately scoured the internet, trying to find recommendations for a repair company. I went back and forth multiple times, weighing different service fees. I got stressed out about which one to hire. I wasn't trying to make the right decision; I was more worried about making the wrong decision. What if I called a company that overcharged me? Or was just plain bad at their job? I finally realized it didn't matter because I would never even know what the alternative would be!

We find this same phenomenon in business. Most people are not focused on finding the best decision. They are attempting to find the one that is least wrong. The result of this fear is often that the best decision is not chosen, and thus we end up with consequences. People are more concerned with not making the wrong choice than with making the right one.

SOCIAL PRESSURE

In my opinion, the most powerful bias we all share is that of social proof. It can cause a normal person to do something they would never consider on their own. There is an extremely famous *Candid Camera* episode from 1962 that illustrates this phenomenon perfectly.

The setup: an individual is riding in an elevator. Several *Candid Camera* employees enter the elevator and face the rear, instead of facing the front doors. The man begins to grow visibly uncomfortable and unsure of what to do. After a moment's hesitation, he turns and faces the back of the elevator. It is a hilarious example of how we as humans would prefer to not stand out and just follow the herd. We will copy what others do even if we don't understand or agree with what they are doing. Even if we look ridiculous!

EXECUTIVE HAMSTER WHEEL

No one gets in trouble for trying to cut costs or automate or "streamline." These are safe choices that shareholders and company boards accept. If their initiative fails, it rarely comes back on them; it was either the fault of the business environment or the people who executed it.

This is ludicrous and blows your mind, but it is a fact of life. The executives got there not by being the best but by playing the game the best. They created an emotional connection and learned how to manage up. They are not immune to bad decisions, but they learned how to navigate the consequences of the fallout.

You can use the same toolkit to get to the next level, or, at the very least, protect your current position. Most executives I have had the pleasure to interact with are not incompetent. None of them has a desire to see the business fail, and there is nothing vindictive about what they do. (Except for that one guy, but that's a story for another time.) They are human and are making decisions with incomplete information and biases intact. They walk into a situation where there are only a few things they can do. Cut costs, re-org, or streamline processes. *That's it.*

You face a *Groundhog Day* scenario every time a new leader comes into the business. They make the same decisions in a different way. Why? Because they don't really know what to do, and they are trying to preserve their career as well. The result is that they go into the grab bag of corporate solutions. "I have decided we have too many people, so we are going to cut the workforce by 10 percent." Really? What magic did you use to come up with that number? Or I should say, how many millions did you pay to outside consultants for them to say that? It's the easy choice. No one gets fired for doing what the $10 million consultants tell them to do.

Just when you get your boss figured out, he will change. Time for a re-org. There is a war on middle managers. You are on the hook for other people's decisions. You are the easiest scapegoat in the business; you *have* to be prepared when they come for you, and they will. But you can beat them; you can outthink them.

I write all this to show you that leaders will continue to make the same mistakes over and over and over again. They will make bad trade-offs in decisions. They will cut the budget and harm productivity. They will focus on the little picture instead of the big one. They will needlessly waste your time on meaningless tasks. The hamster wheel is going to keep turning no matter which hamster jumps on.

BUILD A SHELTER

Here in the South, we have one threat that is guaranteed to strike: tornados. They come with very little warning and can devastate everything in their path. My house is built with a tornado shelter. At the first sign of bad weather, the family runs into that little concrete room and prepares to wait it out. It is stocked full of supplies that will let us survive for days if the need arises.

You need to build a bad-decision shelter, a place where you can safely hide when the insanity comes. You have to be prepared. Understand that no one cares about your career but you. Only you can protect it.

Thursday was layoff day. There was a list being circulated of the names the executives had decided to let go. It was a grim time, to be sure. Thursday came, and the notifications went out. We watched as several employees began to pack up their belongings. Yet several names that were on the original list still sat comfortably. At the last minute, they were saved, even though their group was impacted. They had built a positive relationship with an executive based on past performance, so when their name came up, someone put a stop to it.

No one survives alone; you have to build relationships. The best protection you can have is the relationships you have built, and the more powerful the relationship, the better. If a key executive knows your name, all the better. You get this relationship by following the advice in the previous chapters. Make the emotional impact. Make them remember you. Control the perception battle.

Bosses change so often that you have to be ready to broaden your reach for relationships. Take every opportunity that you can to present in front of other people. Your main goal is name recognition.

Almost everyone has a reactive strategy at work. They sit and wait until they are told to do something, and then they go do it. They sit and wait for things to happen to them. They wonder why they haven't been promoted as they sit and wait for someone to tell them what a good job they are doing. You will fail in this mindset. In order to be prepared for the inevitable stupid decisions, you have to have a proactive career strategy. I will repeat one of the quotes from Jack Welch: "Take control of your destiny or someone else will." This is the very definition of a proactive strategy. You can't sit around and wait for your career to happen. It won't be given to you. You have to take it. You do that by making sure you take every opportunity to stand out. Be the person who asks for more responsibility. Be the person who asks what you can do to help. Be the person who volunteers for the bad project no one wants. If you sit still, you will be unprepared when the insanity comes, and you'll be ignored or unemployed.

You are human. (Well, I guess that depends on when you are reading this—you could potentially be a cyborg by now or something. For the sake of argument, let's say you are human.) What this means is you are prone to the exact same biases and flawed decision-making as the executives you mock. As much as you would like to think you would do a better job, in the same position with the same information, you would likely end up making the same decisions. The only way out of this vicious cycle is to recognize the unconscious biases that you hold and ensure they are not a factor of the decisions you make. Looking at the biases that are commonly held and the self-preservation instinct we all share will help you better predict how someone is going to behave. If you can predict it, then you can manage it. Look for the repeatable patterns in their behavior, and ensure you are not prone to the same ones.

Over the course of your career, you will be asked to execute bad decisions over and over again. You will witness new leaders making the same mistakes and old leaders making new ones. It can be a frustrating situation to be continually placed in. Understanding the myriad ways that these bad decisions get made can help you understand and potentially predict their behavior, and even guard against you one day making the same mistakes.

Like the passersby from the story of the gerbil that opens this chapter, people are focusing on the woman and the man "attacking" her, you need to be on the lookout for the gerbil. Be proactive in getting your name out there, and make sure that when it comes up, they know who you are. The only true way to stop bad decisions is to kill them at the root. You have to be in the room when they are made. Be laser-focused on being known and finding the gerbil, and you will be there one day.

KEY TAKEAWAYS

1. We use our experience bias to make faster decisions.
2. The further away you are from the impacts of that decision, the worse it will be.
3. Everyone will always pick the safest choice.
4. People are scared to make the wrong decision, so they attempt to pick what is the least wrong instead of focusing on what is best.
5. Everyone follows the herd because there is safety in numbers.
6. The same decisions will continue to be made over and over again. There are not many other options available to leadership.
7. Build a shelter of relationships and name recognition in order to survive.
8. The only way to survive is to have a proactive strategy in place.
9. Did you identify the gerbil? Or are you more concerned with what everyone else is doing?

ACTION TO TAKE TODAY

Write down what biases you have. Consult this list when you face your next decision. Are you making the same mistakes?

~~~~~

CHAPTER 9

~~~~~

MANAGE YOURSELF

*I am convinced that life is 10% what happens
to me and 90% how I react to it.*
—CHARLES SWINDOLL

I looked down and saw my boss's name flash across the
caller ID screen. This had to be something important, as
he rarely found the need to actually call me.

"We have a presentation for several VPs tomorrow, and I
need a one-page write-up on all the projects on our team.
Can you please compile this for everyone?" He spoke in
a rushed and excited tone that underscored this was the
most important thing I needed to be doing.

Once we hung up, I realized my day was shot, so I cleared
my calendar. Then I spent the next four hours in Pow-

erPoint jail creating the perfect representation of what our team was working on. I had once heard a story that a bad PowerPoint led to a project not being funded, so we wanted to make sure we got this right.

I went back and forth with many of my peers, and we felt confident in what we were putting together. I pressed send and submitted the file for my boss's approval. Within thirty minutes, I already had a reply asking for multiple revisions. I went right back to work and hit submit on the final version. It was now six o'clock. Time to go home. The meeting came and went, and I never heard anything. Anxious to see how all our hard work had been received, I called my boss to see if there were any questions the VP had on our projects.

"Oh, we never made it to the PowerPoint deck. We ran long on some other topics."

No one ever saw the slides I spent an entire day working on. No one.

How do you maintain sanity when everything around you conspires to drive you mad? Your company will waste your time and your effort constantly and then blame you when things don't go well. One of the key components we haven't touched upon yet is critical: how to manage yourself during this time of stress and uncertainty.

It's true that most of your success will be determined by your focus on the people around you, but remember, another key part is your own mental stability. For someone who cares about their career and reputation, it is hard to accept a project with little chance of success. It is even harder to outright fail. This can have the same negative consequences on your motivation and your attitude as everyone else's. You have to manage yourself.

I am going to give you the same advice that I have given multiple times in multiple settings—focus on what you can control. Every single chapter in this book has focused on things you can control and actions you can take. You can't control your boss, your company's stupid policies, or dumb employees. You do have a choice on how you react to them. How you react in these times is what ultimately will decide the trajectory of your career.

MANAGE YOUR TIME

You will be asked to do more things than you can accomplish or, as the intro story can attest, be asked to do things that are a waste of time. To handle this, you have to make sure you are managing your time effectively. The net result of a lot of terrible decisions is they will waste a lot of your time and resources with very little to show for it. To combat this time-suck, you have to have a surefire method and way to manage your time whenever a request comes. My cousin, Paul Thompson, who dealt with the same corporate insanity, came up with an easy three-question test to accomplish this. When the request of your time comes in, ask yourself these three questions.

1. WHAT WOULD HAPPEN IF I JUST DIDN'T DO THIS?

Would there actually be any real repercussions if you did not complete this task? What is the worst thing that could happen if you didn't do this? If there would be real consequences, then you have no choice but to do it. You would be surprised how many tasks can't get by this first question.

I have a pretty good example of this. Every week, we were supposed to email our status reports. Just a nice bullet-point list of everything we were working on. We'd email it to one of the folks on another team, then they would compile it together—build a little email newsletter and send it over to our executive director. It took me about an hour a week to put this together, but I had the sneaking suspicion nobody was reading them. I wondered what would happen if I just didn't send in my update. So I didn't. And nothing happened. I didn't send it in for an entire year before someone said something. A year. I saved myself fifty-two hours. Because it couldn't even get past the first question.

2. COULD THIS BE AUTOMATED?

Is this a request of you that happens more than once? Is it a PowerPoint or report you could easily build into a macro? Think about creative ways to reduce the amount of time it takes to handle recurring requests.

We launched a new product, and everyone wanted all these metrics and stat reports. The requests would come from a bunch of different groups, but the information would end up being the same. We built a quick script we could run to pull in the stats and spit out a nicely formatted report. Every time we got asked that question, we just pushed a button and it was done.

3. CAN THIS BE DELEGATED?

Is there someone else on your team who could do an equal or better job than you? Trust your team with some of these assignments so you can focus on the larger issues at hand. Your team is smarter than you and better than you at most tasks.

This third question is not about dumping tasks you just don't want to do on other people; it is about understanding if someone could do a better job than you. If they can have a better output than you, if it takes less time, and if it has a better result, then that is a more efficient use of resources.

If a task can pass these three questions, then you know it is something you need to focus on. You can save yourself a huge amount of time over your career by examining the asks of your time. Go take a look at your current to-do list and ask these questions of each one. I am going to bet at least one of those items can be removed after reviewing this. Give it a week and view your work through a different lens.

THE KEY TO SANITY

I walked into the conference room and sat at one of the biggest round tables I had ever seen. I was surrounded by executives on all sides. It was almost like I had just entered the room with Arthur and the knights of the Round Table. As I took my seat, they all glanced up from their laptops and just stared at me. Their gazes all had a quizzical look: "Who are you?"

The last five months of my life was all leading up to this moment. I had been working on a Six Sigma project for process improvements in our inventory control. During my research, I had uncovered $30 million in equipment that had been missed and could have been put into service sooner. It was time to present my conclusions for the project on how we could improve. I cleared my throat and stood. I went through my PowerPoint deck with the skill of a seasoned pro as the executives looked on. As I drew to a dramatic conclusion, I outlined the new process steps that were needed to ensure this error didn't happen again. As I finished, I felt proud; I had done a great job and presented my case well. Five months of work well spent. The vice president looked up and down at my PowerPoint for a final time and then spoke.

"This looks good. I am glad you found the error, but we are not going to implement any of these steps."

I stood in shock, not sure how to proceed. Had I messed up? Did I miss one of my points? I attempted to defend my conclusion. They all agreed my conclusions were correct, but it was not something they wanted to implement. No logic, no reasoning, they just said no. Five months of work for nothing. I walked out of the conference room in shock, still not fully comprehending what had just happened. Why did they not want to take my recommendations? It just didn't make any sense. It was in that moment I knew. I was completely at the mercy of other people's ridiculous decisions.

The key to sanity when working for a corporation is to expect the absurd. Do not approach a situation with normal logic. Start with the opposite of what you think should be done and approach it from there. There are hundreds of decisions and policies that you will come across in your career that will not make sense. Your leadership will make trade-offs and policies you do not agree with. If you let them, they will slowly chip away at you, leaving nothing but a cynical core. The hardest challenge is that these things stick with you and pile up over time if you don't find a way to wash away the absurd you deal with every day.

How do you not let these things affect you? The key is to make sure you completely unplug at the end of the day. The brain is a fairly predictable thing. It enjoys routines and habits. It likes to be comfortable. You need to create an end-of-day habit that signals the workday is over and it's okay to shift to other responsibilities. It can be as simple as listening to a specific song or going for a run. The point is to make sure you have a specific trigger you can hit each day that signals to your brain that work is over.

I have a specific routine I do every day that helps me transition into something new, and it unburdens me of things that might bother me that night. At the end of my workday, I grab a final cup of coffee and make a to-do list for the next day. A list of everything I need to accomplish tomorrow. This is a mental exercise of purging everything that is in my head and work-related. As a side effect, it actually helps start my next day better as well. Once this list is done, I shut my computer down and head home. I know that once the computer is shut down, so is my work for the day. You will be surprised how effective this can be. Find a routine that works for you that helps you transition to a new part of the day.

The objections I normally see to this involve the use of smartphones and the always-connected crowd. It's true I have been called at night and have had work emergencies to take care of, but most of the time, the after-hours emails can be taken care of the next day with absolutely no impact on anyone. Try to keep that in mind when you feel the itch to check your work email. Turn those notifications off. I am going to guess you are not curing cancer, so whatever Excel spreadsheet is needed can wait until tomorrow. You're not that important.

It's easy to get wrapped up in the pace and intensity of your job. Everything you get assigned or told about is the most important thing in the world and needs to be done right away. Is it really, though? Take a step back and run everything through the three questions. Is it actually worth your time to do it? Would your career actually be hampered if it didn't get done immediately? Almost always, the answer will be no. Not only do you need to protect your time, but you have to protect your sanity as well. You must find a way to unplug and signal that the day is over. The stress and insanity of work *will* build up and overwhelm you over time if you do not find a way to clear it out each day. Find that routine to signal that it is time to move on. If you take care of yourself first, you will find it is easier to take care of your team and take care of your career. You might even survive the insanity.

KEY TAKEAWAYS

1. You have to guard your time.
   a. What would happen if I just didn't do this?
   b. Could this be automated?
   c. Can this be delegated?
2. You have to find a way to leave work at work.
3. Create an end-of-the day habit to trigger to your brain that work is over.

ACTION TO TAKE TODAY

Make a list of all your tasks and run them through the three rules. Develop an end-of-day routine.

CHAPTER 10

CONCLUSION

It is remarkable how much long-term advantage
people like us have gotten by trying to be consistently
not stupid, instead of trying to be very intelligent.
—CHARLIE MUNGER

I was the manager of a software development team. We were actively working on building an enterprise-scale tool that could digest huge amounts of data and serve the demands of a lot of teams within our company. If that means nothing to you, just understand it was really hard.

We had a lot of users to listen to and many demands on our time. My boss, who was a hardened thirty-year veteran of the industry, called me one day and let me know that, due to a company reorganization, in addition to my current role, I would be given another new software project to take over. This gift would come with seven additional people to manage, and to top it off, the project was over a year behind schedule.

I was, of course, concerned because I already had a full-time job, and this was just going to make even more demands of my time. Did I mention the best part was that this project came with an unrealistic deadline that would be impossible to meet? This was a no-win situation. I was being set up to fail due to someone else's bad decision. I had to lean on the techniques we have already discussed in order to navigate and mitigate the consequences.

Let's review:

1. STOP wasting your energy trying to make other people smarter.
2. FOCUS on making your boss successful.
3. ALIGN yourself with your team.
4. CONTROL the narrative.
5. DECIDE what emotional impact to convey.
6. DON'T BE AN IDIOT.
7. PREPARE for the inevitable.
8. MANAGE yourself.

When looking at these steps, it doesn't seem to be too challenging. Let's put them together, shall we?

1. I didn't spend my time trying to convince my boss that this was an unrealistic demand. The decision had been made; what good would it do? However, I did state my concerns, and I phrased it exactly like this: "This looks like a good opportunity; I think we can be successful with this project. It will, however, divert my attention off of my current project." I was very clear what the trade-offs and the potential impact of this new project would be.

2. I also asked him plainly, "What are your success criteria for this project?" What was his measurement to be successful? Once we had that established, it was time to tell the team. In this example, there were some additional metrics to hit for usage, but the key was to hit the deadline, something I already knew would not be possible.

3. "Yes, this is going to be a challenge, but we were chosen because we are so good at what we do. They have confidence that we can succeed where others have failed." They were not exactly thrilled, but now they had something to prove. After an initial assessment, I determined that the project was in even worse shape than I could have thought possible. We were going to have to throw away huge chunks of the code and rewrite. What's worse, as I already mentioned, the executive leadership had decided to set an arbitrary date. We had to be finished with our work just three months in the future. Without talking to

any of the actual developers on the project, they had decided on an aggressive timeline that had no relevance other than a number on a calendar. Now it was time to control the narrative. I knew I would fail.

4. "We have diverted all resources to this effort, and we are tracking to the August date but are currently facing these X issues." I overcommunicated like crazy! Weekly emails and calls. I kept my boss apprised of progress at least every other day.

5. How would I be remembered for this project? The guy who overpromised? The complainer? No. I made a conscious decision to have a positive attitude. Let me tell you, that is not my normal temperament. The struggle was real. Every call with my boss, I communicated the challenges, but I made sure to end on a positive note. "But we are making great progress and I am really pleased with how hard the team is working."

6. We failed. Despite our best efforts, we did not hit our original deadline. This was not a surprise to anyone because we had communicated and signaled it well in advance. We missed it by a full month, which in hindsight was itself incredible. I put together a comprehensive after-action report that included two large sections: the issues that slowed us down and what steps we could take to make sure we improved delivery speed next time. I controlled the narrative.

7. The aftermath: I was extremely stressed out about

missing that date. But once I did, not much happened. They were disappointed, sure, but because I had indicated all the issues and, even more, had provided the steps needed to fix them, it was very difficult for them to point fingers at our team. I had made them part of the entire progress.

8. Even though I knew the likelihood for success was low, it hurt to fail. The truth is I knew we had done everything possible, but it was not a winnable scenario. The hardest thing is to just move on, but that's what I did. I did my end-of-day ritual as always, shut down my computer, and got ready to start the next day.

As the story illustrates, it's not as hard as it would seem to navigate a bad decision or potential failure. As irrational as people are, they are still predictable. Taking the steps I have laid out will guarantee that the impact of executing someone else's bad call will be as minimal as possible.

WHERE DOES THE PROBLEM LIE?

I am going to get a little philosophical on you now. Your boss and the company are not the problem. It is you. The thing that can sabotage your career more than any bad decision you can face is going to be you and your expectations. Your attitude can and will hold you back.

So often I see employees get burned out, get frustrated, and quit because they do not approach work with the right attitude. They bounce around from job to job and company to company, searching for fulfillment that they won't find. What they are searching for, they can find within themselves.

I know that is a little deep, but stay with me for a moment. You have to find your way through all the frustrations and come out the other end. If you can honestly say you have done everything you could to be successful in this job, then you can think about doing something else. Corporate work is hard and frustrating. You can only be guaranteed that you will be overworked and under-appreciated. You will be asked to do things that defy all common sense, but you can get through this. The corporate world can also be extremely rewarding, and a large company is going to give you access to a huge network of great people. No doubt you have heard the expression "Life is what you make it." The same mantra holds true of your career as well. Make a choice to be successful and then follow the things that I have laid out in this book when dumb things around you happen.

> "If you don't like something, change it. If you can't change it, change your attitude"
> —MAYA ANGELOU

Your career path is not linear. Anyone who has tried to climb the corporate ladder at some point can tell you this same thing. You will have lateral moves and sometimes feel like you have moved backward. It doesn't seem to make sense. You have to trust the process and your own work. Your career is what you make it.

I was given an opportunity to talk with Scott Adams, the creator of *Dilbert*. As someone who has made a career by making fun of the chaos of corporate America and the silliness of the boss, he is uniquely qualified to give a perspective on dealing with idiots. He also understands the frustration that comes with working with them. Our first inclination is to jump ship and try to find a better job, but the truth is, as he put it, "There are no people that do not have issues; you learn to just go with it. If you leave here, you will just talk to other idiots. Ends up being the same. Everything is broken, which is a weird relief."

There is the sad but comforting truth. There are idiots everywhere; they will be at every company you deal with. Running somewhere else isn't going to solve the problem. You have to deal with the idiots everywhere, so everything else being equal, it might as well be here. Life is more about moving forward—not to a destination but in a general direction.

> "Life is hard. You will always feel you are in the right direction if you are learning something. What you learn is who you are."
>
> —SCOTT ADAMS

Keep your focus not on the mistakes of others but on yourself. Move yourself forward by making sure you are learning every day. The good news is you get to learn a lot from other people's mistakes. In the moment, I never appreciated this. As I look back, I see the lessons I learned from presenting wrong conclusions to a bunch of VPs, or the time I ran a project that failed. Your success will be in the cumulative experience of successes and failures.

DON'T BE THE PROBLEM

We have talked in this book about how to manage the bad decisions that you are forced to execute on a daily basis, but how do you actually stop them? You already learned in Chapter 1 all about the futility of trying to change someone's mind. The only way to stop the flow of bad ideas is to be in the room when they start to grow. You have to kill them at the root.

One of the privileges of my first management position was that I was one of the few managers who was able to regularly attend directors-only meetings. This was an eye-opening experience. To hear some of the things they talked about was interesting and somewhat disturbing. I distinctly remember sitting in the back of the room when one of the directors stood up and talked about how much he didn't like remote employees and would never hire one. Then he went on to complain about how he couldn't find any qualified candidates, because everyone was too spoiled to move states for him. There was the time we were told to inflate all our budget numbers because we knew HQ was required to make cuts. They look good, so we look good. The list goes on and on. You have to be in those meetings to be able to stop the bad idea from spreading. Take the advice given in the previous chapters and apply it. Make sure you are around to make the leap to the next level, but be prepared—the insanity only seems to intensify as you move up.

The challenge is that the higher you move up the corporate ladder, the more convinced you are of your own greatness. It is your own personal form of confirmation bias. You have been successful, so your decisions must be good, right? You begin to trust yourself more than the things around you, and you fall into the *exact* same trap you swore you would never be in. The people who work for you are now reading this book because they think you are an idiot. It is important to spot-check yourself.

> Michael: "What was the most inspiring thing I've ever said to you?"
>
> Dwight: "'Don't be an idiot.' Changed my life."
>
> —*THE OFFICE*

Recognize what happens when you are the one who is wrong. Focus on the things in these chapters that you can use to keep from being the problem. The only way we can fix corporate culture is if we get enough people in power who understand where the insanity comes from. You can make a difference. Make sure you take out Chapter 7 and reread it once a year just to give yourself a gut check to know where you went wrong. Give this book to other people. Don't become the same thing that you are fighting against!

It is possible to fail miserably and have a great career. It is possible to outlive a bad decision or a bad boss. The key is to know how to navigate the people who are around it. Your career will not be made up of the results you achieve but by how you manage the people around you. I hope you got something of value out of this book. I know I found value in writing it. The bad decisions and crazy people are going to keep coming. You are not alone in dealing with this insanity. We all have to suffer through this, but we can get through it. Good luck, and remember the reward for good work is just more work.

I love crazy corporate stories. Have something to share or want to ask a question? Email me at Donald@corporatemiddle.com.

For more info, go check out TheCorporateMiddle.com.

ABOUT THE AUTHOR

Donald has survived mergers, promotions, reorganizations, and downsizing. Throughout his career, he has led multiple technical teams of varying sizes consisting of both on- and offshore resources. He has successfully led multi-million-dollar projects and was selected to complete a two-year program to become a Certified Lean Six Sigma Black Belt. Donald has a degree in computer engineering and an MBA. In addition to his corporate experience, he has cofounded multiple companies. Donald is an award-winning speaker and the host of the podcast *The Corporate Middle*, where he answers the most common middle-management questions. For more information, check out DonaldMeador.com.

Made in the USA
Monee, IL
22 September 2020